REDISCOVERING
THE
GLORY
OF THE
SABBATH

JO ANN DAVIDSON

Pacific Press®
Publishing Association

Nampa, Idaho | www.pacificpress.com

Cover design by Gerald Lee Monks
Cover design resources from iStockphoto.com | Nongkran_ch
Inside design by Aaron Troia

The author assumes full responsibility for the accuracy of all facts and quotations as cited in this book.

Unless otherwise indicated, all Scripture quotations are taken from the New King James Version®. Copyright © 1982 by Thomas Nelson. Used by permission. All rights reserved.

Scripture quotations marked KJV are from the King James Version of the Bible.

Scripture quotations marked RSV are from the Revised Standard Version of the Bible, copyright © 1946, 1952, 1971 by the Division of Christian Education of the National Council of the Churches of Christ in the USA. Used by permission.

Additional copies of this book are available for purchase by calling toll-free 1-800-765-6955 or by visiting AdventistBookCenter.com.

Library of Congress Cataloging-in-Publication Data

Names: Davidson, Jo Ann, author.
Title: Rediscovering the Glory of the Sabbath / Jo Ann Davidson.
Description: Nampa, Idaho : Pacific Press Publishing Association, 2020. |
    Summary: "An exploration of the history of the Sabbath revealing it as God's
    invitation to blessing and delight"— Provided by publisher.
Identifiers: LCCN 2020028652 (print) | LCCN 2020028653 (ebook) |
    ISBN 9780816366651 | ISBN 9780816366668 (ebook edition)
Subjects: LCSH: Sabbath. | General Conference of Seventh-Day Adventists—
    Doctrines.
Classification: LCC BV125 .D286 2020 (print) | LCC BV125 (ebook) | DDC
    263/.2—dc23
LC record available at https://lccn.loc.gov/2020028652
LC ebook record available at https://lccn.loc.gov/2020028653

January 2021

Dedication

This book is dedicated to Dr. Jay and Nancy Crawford, my beloved sister and brother-in-law, whose warm and generous Sabbath hospitality has blessed so many with joy and rest.

Contents

Introduction | *7*
First Things First

Chapter 1 | *15*
Back to the Beginning

Chapter 2 | *56*
The Sabbath in Old Testament History and Song

Chapter 3 | *93*
The Intertestamental Period: What Happened?

Chapter 4 | *113*
The Lord of the Sabbath: His Day and His Disciples

Chapter 5 | *155*
After the New Testament: What Happened?

Chapter 6 | *183*
What's the Problem?

Chapter 7 | *198*
The Heart of the Matter

Introduction

First Things First

The Sabbath has always been a central issue for the Seventh-day Adventist Church, so much so that it is part of our denominational name. We are "seventh-day" Adventists, separating us from others who also believe in the second coming of Jesus but do not link it to the biblical Sabbath.

A book looking into the biblical Sabbath will interest some but will arouse no interest at all for others. Some may have their curiosity tweaked, but for many Christians today, the study of any biblical doctrine is unappealing. They find pursuing those studies boring and pedantic. They think, *It may have been necessary to study doctrines in the past, but not now.* They seek relational models of Christian identity, models that emphasize the love of Jesus or make a person more "spiritual." Still others find the church and its doctrines unnecessary. They feel that they enjoy greater blessings and benefits in nature. Moreover, church leaders can't seem to agree on many doctrinal issues anyway.

Studying anything, however, involves making choices, whether it is religion, politics, philosophy, or learning a skill. Ideas and beliefs matter, and every person must decide what is true. Not choosing is itself making a choice. There is no neutral ground. Even pluralism, which urges tolerance, is a commitment to certain assumptions. And the tolerance urged there ends when someone does not accept the pluralistic platform.

Rediscovering the Glory the Sabbath

Christian faith has never been about merely gathering the best combination of texts—though sometimes it may seem so. It is about encountering, loving, and wanting to serve the living God. To know Him, a person must find where and how He has revealed Himself. Which, of course, involves studying Scripture, the primary source for that revelation. Such study involves accepting Scripture's claims about itself: that though there were many writers, God was the Author. Furthermore, all the biblical writers illuminate each other. There is no instance in which one writer contradicts or proves another wrong. Scripture can be trusted. Ellen White is passionate about this: "The Bible is its own interpreter. With beautiful simplicity, one portion connects itself with the truth of another portion, until the whole Bible is blended in one harmonious whole. Light flashes forth from one text to illuminate some portion of the Word that has seemed more obscure."[1]

The purpose of this book is not to defend the inspired nature of Scripture, but it is rightly assumed. With this assumption comes the all-important reminder that studying biblical doctrine is not merely lining up all the right texts. Nevertheless, the entire biblical canon must be studied—for it is a complete system of truth.

In the following pages, it will be seen that the Sabbath is a major biblical topic—and it is intertwined with other such biblical doctrines as the doctrine of God, the doctrine of humanity, the covenant, the doctrine of salvation, the great controversy between Christ and Satan, and more. As with all doctrinal studies, each link is crucial, intersecting and holding together a golden "chain of truth." Ellen White explains more than once the importance of Scripture's "chain of truth": "The grand truths of sacred history possess amazing strength and beauty, and are as far-reaching as eternity. What more important knowledge can be gained than that which outlines the fall of man and the consequences of that sin, which opened the floodgates of woe upon the world, which tells of Christ's first advent? The incarnation of Christ, His divinity,

His atonement, His wonderful life in heaven as our advocate, the office of the Holy Spirit—all these vital themes of Christianity are revealed from Genesis to Revelation. Each is a golden link in the perfect chain of truth."[2]

Connected questions concerning the Sabbath are, Is the Sabbath related to salvation? Is keeping it a requirement for being saved? Or is it more important to become more "spiritual"?

Even the quest for answers to these questions can be dangerous if not grounded biblically. As the apostle Paul instructs: "Do not quench the Spirit. Do not despise prophecies. *Test all things*; hold fast what is good. Abstain from every form of evil" (1 Thessalonians 5:19–22; emphasis added). To "test" something, there must be a standard. And that standard is the Bible. With the divine Author authenticating His Word, we know it can be trusted. And all sixty-six books are necessary. Each one teaches, informs, and corresponds with the others.

Christian faith is not based on a set of mystical, ill-defined, or unclear ideas about the world and its inhabitants. Nor is it a casual collection of Bible writers recording their intuitive emotions about spiritual matters. From Genesis to Revelation, the teachings of Scripture cluster around and focus on Jesus. The sixty-six books begin with Him as the masterful Lord of Creation week (Genesis 1; 2; Colossians 1:3, 4, 16–18) and climax with the book entitled "The Revelation of Jesus Christ."

At the heart of Christian faith is a Person, not a dry doctrine. And when people want to study and share what they know about Jesus, they are dealing with doctrine. Recall Jesus' own testimony about the Old Testament—on Resurrection Sunday, no less. Traveling on the road to Emmaus, He met up with two disciples who were grieving about Jesus having died that weekend. As He joined their conversation, He did not triumphantly announce His presence—which would have been the easiest way to bring exceeding joy to the grieving disciples. He first turned their minds to the Old Testament Scriptures: "Then He said to them, 'O foolish ones, and slow of heart to believe in all that the prophets have spoken! Ought not the Christ to have suffered these things and to enter into His glory?' And *beginning at Moses and all the Prophets, He expounded to them in all the Scriptures the things concerning Himself*" (Luke 24:25–27; emphasis added).

Responding to that discussion later in their home, as they recalled what Jesus had explained to them, the disciples marveled: "Did not our heart burn within us while He talked with us on the road, and while He opened the Scriptures to us?" (verse 32). In fact, it wrought such a profound change in their thinking that they had to dash back to Jerusalem and encourage the other despondent disciples with what they had learned.

Jesus then graciously reappeared among them all—and reiterated the same biblical principle that had caused the "burning heart" experience in Emmaus. "Then He said to them, 'These are the *words which I spoke* to you while I was still with you, that *all things must be fulfilled which were written in the Law of Moses and the Prophets and the Psalms concerning Me.*' And *He opened their understanding, that they might comprehend the Scriptures*" (verses 44, 45; emphasis added).

Jesus' opening "their understanding, that they might comprehend the Scriptures" emphasizes that Scripture is a system of truth. And since Jesus is none other than God Incarnate, His teaching has authority and weight. This makes it clear that when we study the Bible, we can be blessed with the knowledge of the true God.

Christians do not believe that Jesus has authority because of the excellence and truth of His teaching. Human thinking and evaluation are not needed to establish His authority. He has absolute authority because He is God Incarnate. Our thinking and teaching continually need to be judged by Him.

This book will explore the truth about God through the study of the Sabbath in Scripture. It will, of course, include whether there is a right day and a right time. But more important, behind all the discussion, it portrays the "Lord of the Sabbath."

Seventh-day Adventists have, using both the Old and New Testaments, rightly focused on which day is the correct biblical Sabbath. However, there is much more to discovering the true Sabbath than just knowing the right day. Its glorious nature needs to be restored!

The following chapters will explore and review just how extensively the Sabbath is highlighted and embedded in the Bible from Genesis to Revelation—sometimes explicitly, often implicitly. They will make it obvious that the doctrine of the Sabbath is not a peripheral or minor issue, nor have we been following "cunningly devised fables." After that, a brief survey of the Sabbath in history will recount how the Sabbath was never lost, and a few supposed "problem Sabbath texts" will be investigated. The concluding chapter once more highlights the Sabbath by celebrating its glorious nature and includes some practical ideas to enhance its observance.

Our study begins as Genesis opens and follows through the next sixty-five canonical books until the canon closes. The historical books contribute as does the book of Psalms—the "official hymnal" for Old Testament sanctuary worship. Even the "penitential psalms," especially linked to Yom Kippur in the seventh month of Israel's ritual calendar, are important because the Day of Atonement was called the "high Sabbath" or the "greater Sabbath." And thus, those psalms are a vital part of any Sabbath theology.

Some of the Old Testament prophets mentioned the Sabbath by name as they sought its restoration to Sabbath keepers who were keeping the right day the wrong way. The prophet Isaiah, quoting the Lord, provides major proof that the Sabbath is not just for the Jews but is for all people. "All peoples" are described with two characteristics: honoring the covenant and keeping the Sabbath:

For thus says the LORD:

Rediscovering the Glory the Sabbath

"To the eunuchs who keep My Sabbaths,
And choose what pleases Me,
And hold fast My covenant,
Even to them I will give in My house
And within My walls a place and a name
Better than that of sons and daughters;
I will give them an everlasting name
That shall not be cut off.

"Also the sons of the foreigner
Who join themselves to the LORD, to serve Him,
And to love the name of the LORD, to be His servants—
Everyone who keeps from defiling the Sabbath,
And holds fast My covenant—
Even them I will bring to My holy mountain,
And make them joyful in My house of prayer" (Isaiah
    56:4–7).

The Old Testament Israelites were given divine instructions on what was ethically normative for God's people: the Sabbath was identified as a vital posture of fellowship with Him.

In chapter 58, Isaiah also spoke of Sabbath restoration, quoting the divine promise that this would bring "delight"!

"If you turn away your foot from the Sabbath,
From doing your pleasure on My holy day,
And call the *Sabbath a delight*,
The holy day of the LORD honorable,
And shall honor Him, not doing your own ways,
Nor finding your own pleasure,
Nor speaking your own words,
Then you shall delight yourself in the LORD;
And I will cause you to ride on the high hills of the earth,

And feed you with *the heritage of Jacob your father*.
The mouth of the LORD has spoken" (verses 13, 14; emphasis
   added).

This passage reminds us that the Sabbath was never meant to be
a burden or a restriction. Instead, it is a cause for delight!

Later, when taken into captivity, the prophet Ezekiel admonished the Israelites that their apostasy had been caused by their
desecration of the Sabbath (Ezekiel 20). Following their return
from Babylonian captivity, the importance of Sabbath to the divine
Creator was urged by the prophet Nehemiah (Nehemiah 13).
And Nehemiah, like Ezekiel, reminded them that violation of the
Sabbath was what led to their captivity in Babylon (verses 17–19).

A pattern can be detected in Old Testament history: The Sabbath
was taught, perverted, and restored more than once. However, the
Sabbath is never called "Jewish" anywhere in Scripture. It was
instituted thousands of years before there were any Jews. Jesus
also insisted that "the Sabbath was made for *man*"—not for just
a certain ethnic group (Mark 2:27, 28). There were drastic results
for humans and all creation because of sin's entrance—but the
Sabbath was given before sin, and it was not changed after sin.

The New Testament depicts Jesus keeping the Sabbath, "as
His custom was" (Luke 4:16). In the book of Acts, the apostles
are shown keeping the Sabbath. Paul also kept the Sabbath, and
several times in his letters to the Gentile churches he had established, he refers to the Decalogue, even quoting from the fourth
commandment in one of his prayers.

As the canon closes in the book of Revelation, a glorious future
is promised. At last, the curse and results of sin will be removed—
and "a new heaven and a new earth" (Revelation 21:1) will be
created. And it will be such a glorious time that God can't help
but refer to it in the Old Testament through Isaiah, where He
promised that the blessing of the Sabbath would continue:

Rediscovering the Glory the Sabbath

"For as the new heavens and the new earth
Which I will make shall remain before Me," says the LORD,
"So shall your descendants and your name remain.
And it shall come to pass
That from one New Moon to another,
And from one Sabbath to another,
All flesh shall come to worship before Me," says the LORD
(Isaiah 66:22, 23).

The biblical promises of heaven never suggest a disembodied, ethereal, timeless existence. Instead, the very real created world described in Genesis 1 and 2 is promised to be restored—and the biblical Sabbath will continue! The Creator's dreams for this planet will finally be realized—and the blessing of the Sabbath will be part of it.

The study of the biblical Sabbath need not be restricted to the fourth commandment of the Decalogue (Exodus 20:8–11). It is linked to

- the Creation of this world,
- redemption,
- its needed restoration,
- the covenant, and
- eschatology, the study of "last things," including final judgment.

A survey of the biblical Sabbath lies ahead—a journey full of joy and fellowship with the Lord of the Sabbath.

---

1. Ellen G. White, *Our High Calling* (Washington, DC: Review and Herald®, 1961), 207.

2. Ellen G. White, *Counsels to Parents, Teachers, and Students* (Mountain View, CA: Pacific Press®, 1943), 427.

Chapter One

Back to the Beginning

The Old Testament—and the Bible itself—opens with the dramatic narration of the day-by-day creation of this world. The literary pattern of the Genesis 1:1–2:3 Creation account serves to highlight the extraordinary event Creation week was. In the first three days, there is (1) the bestowing of light, (2) a separation of firmament and water, and (3) emergence of dry land. The next three days, each of these three "habitats" is filled: (4) sun, moon, and stars filled the light sources; (5) the birds and sea creatures are created and blessed—filling the air and waters; (6) humans and land animals are created and given the same blessing of the birds and sea creatures as they fill their habitat on the newly created soil.

The Creator, well-pleased, declared all of it "very good"—fully delighting in the material world He crafted. "God looked out onto the freshly made creation and saw reflected back in sensual form the full display of his own love, joy, creativity, playfulness, and curiosity. Nothing in creation had to be. . . . But all of it remains precious, the expression of divine poetry, and the exhibition of a passionate Word. . . . For creation to cease to exist, God would have to desist from loving, because it is only God's joyful, creative speech and warm, sustaining breath (see Psalm 104) that daily enlivens and maintains each and every creature."[1]

Ellen White writes similarly: "Our Father in heaven is constantly engaged in upholding the things which He has created. Every leaf grows, every flower blooms, every fruit develops, by the power of God. In Him 'we live, and move, and have our being.' Each heart-beat, each breath, is the inspiration of Him who breathed into the nostrils of Adam the breath of life,—the inspiration of the ever-present God, the great I AM. The great and infinite God lives not unto Himself, but for the benefit and blessing of every being and every object of His creation."[2]

The climactic seventh day follows next. That very first singular week culminated in the creation of twenty-four hours of blessed, holy time. More verbs are linked with the creation of this day than for any of the preceding six—for the Creator "finished," "rested," "blessed," and "sanctified" this final day of the first week. And on the seventh day, unlike the other six, the Creator *both* formed and filled it. The verbs describing His actions indicate He was fully present on the seventh day as He blessed and sanctified it. Elsewhere in the Old Testament, when God sanctifies something— setting it apart, such as the later constructed sanctuary—it is signaled by His glorious presence. "And it came to pass, when the priests came out of the holy place, that the cloud filled the house of the LORD, so that the priests could not continue ministering because of the cloud; for the glory of the LORD filled the house of the LORD" (1 Kings 8:10, 11).

Marriage was also created that first week. He had already blessed all the creatures He had made.

> Then God said, "Let the waters abound with an abundance of living creatures, and let birds fly above the earth across the face of the firmament of the heavens." So God created great sea creatures and every living thing that moves, with which the waters abounded, according to their kind, and every winged bird according to its kind. And God saw that it was good. *And God blessed them*, saying, "Be fruitful and multiply, and fill the waters in the seas, and let birds multiply

on the earth." So the evening and the morning were the fifth day (Genesis 1:20–23; emphasis added).

Then, on the sixth day, marriage was given to Adam and Eve, and it was also blessed by the Creator.

Then God said, "Let Us make man in Our image, according to Our likeness; let them have dominion over the fish of the sea, over the birds of the air, and over the cattle, over all the earth and over every creeping thing that creeps on the earth." So God created man in His own image; in the image of God He created him; male and female He created them. *Then God blessed them*, and God said to them, "Be fruitful and multiply; fill the earth and subdue it; have dominion over the fish of the sea, over the birds of the air, and over every living thing that moves on the earth" (Genesis 1:26–28; emphasis added).

Then God blessed the Sabbath. The Sabbath was instituted before the Fall, just as was marriage. Hence the Sabbath is no more Jewish than is marriage—both are gifts from Eden. Ellen White reminds us, "There were two institutions founded in Eden that were not lost in the fall, the Sabbath and the marriage relation. These were carried by man beyond the gates of paradise. He who loves and observes the Sabbath, and maintains the purity of the marriage institution, thereby proves himself the friend of man and the friend of God."[3] She also writes, "Marriage was from the creation, constituted by God, a divine ordinance. The marriage institution was made in Eden. The Sabbath of the fourth commandment was instituted in Eden, when the foundations of the world were laid, when the morning stars sang together, and all the sons of God shouted for joy. Then let this, God's institution of marriage, stand before you as firm as the Sabbath of the fourth commandment."[4]

The Sabbath day could not be endowed with more glory. Ellen

Rediscovering the Glory the Sabbath

White points out that it even has a protective nature:

> God gave the Sabbath as a memorial of his creative power and works, "for in six days the Lord made heaven and earth, the sea, and all that in them is, and rested the seventh day; wherefore the Lord blessed the Sabbath day, and hallowed it." He made its observance obligatory upon man, in order that he might contemplate the works of God, dwell upon his goodness, his mercy, and love, and through nature look up to nature's God. *If man had always observed the Sabbath, there would never have been an unbeliever, an infidel, or an atheist in the world.*[5]

Some have argued that the verses describing the creation of the seventh day do not include the "numbering formula" of the previous six days: "the evening and the morning were the [x] day." Because of this, it is suggested that the seventh day is of a different character, such as denoting unending time. However, each of the first six days has *two* numbering formulas. And the wording of Genesis 2:1–3, describing the creation of the first Sabbath, does contain the second of the two "numbering formulas," which was attached to the other six days. The numbering of all seven days was introduced with the definite article—"*the* first day" (Genesis 1:5)," "*the* second day" (Genesis 1:7), "*the* third day" (Genesis 1:13), and so forth. This second "numbering formula" is connected to all seven days. And when it comes to the seventh day in Genesis 2:1–3, the phrase is repeated three times!

"Thus the heavens and the earth, and all the host of them, were finished. And on *the seventh day* God ended His work which He had done, and He rested on *the seventh day* from all His work which He had done. Then God blessed *the seventh day* and sanctified it, because in it He rested from all His work which God had created and made" (Genesis 2:1–3; emphasis added).

Moreover, each mention of "the seventh day" occurs approximately in the middle of three consecutive sentences in the original language. And each of these three sentences has seven words. Through this impressive narrative writing, "the seventh day" is linked with the previous six days—yet it is done so in such a way as to make clear that the seventh day *is* different: not in length but in nature. As Genesis opens, Deity is presented as creating all life and matter. Furthermore, He sets a weekly cycle as He enters and participates in time. Thus, the Sabbath is granted paramount importance: "God is the focus and center of the whole creation account. His activities are stressed. He speaks, acts, and is in control. He is a Sovereign Creator. Eleven times God directly speaks in the first creation story: ten times with the specific formula, 'and God said.' . . . God is explicitly mentioned thirty-five times in thirty-four verses of the first creation story. There is no doubt that God is presented as the Center and the sole Creator."[6]

Moreover, a careful study can hardly miss the extensive use of the number seven in Genesis chapter one.[7] For example, Ivan Panin carefully examined the Hebrew text of Genesis 1:1 and discovered an incredible phenomenon of multiples of seven that could not be explained by chance. For example, Genesis 1:1 ("In the beginning God created the heavens and the earth.") is composed of seven Hebrew words containing a total of 28 (7 × 4) letters. Panin then added up thirty separate codes involving the number seven in the first verse of the Bible. A partial listing includes:

- Genesis 1:1 contains seven Hebrew words.
- The number of letters equals twenty-eight (7 × 4 = 28).
- The first three Hebrew words (translated "in the beginning God created") have fourteen letters (7 × 2 = 14).
- The last four Hebrew words ("the heavens and the earth") have fourteen letters (7 × 2 = 14).

- The fourth and fifth words have seven letters.
- The sixth and seventh words have seven letters.
- The three key words: "God," "heaven," and "earth" have fourteen letters (7 × 2 = 14).
- The number of letters in the four remaining words is also fourteen (7 × 2 = 14).
- The shortest word in the verse is the middle word with seven letters.

The mathematical faculty at Harvard University were presented with this biblical phenomenon. They then attempted to disprove its significance as a proof of divine authorship. Using the English language, they artificially assigned numeric values to the English alphabet—giving them a potential vocabulary of over four hundred thousand available English words to choose from to construct a sentence about any topic they chose. But even after valiant efforts, the professors were unable to duplicate this incredible mathematical phenomenon. Despite their skilled mathematical abilities and computer access, they were unable to come close to incorporating numerous multiples of seven, as found in the Hebrew words of Genesis 1:1.

Beyond the seven days of Creation in Genesis—after God rests, blesses, and sanctifies the seventh day—throughout the rest of the Bible, the numeral seven also reappears many times:

- It appears 287 times in the Old Testament (7 × 41 = 287).
- The word *seventh* occurs ninety-eight times (7 × 14 = 98).
- The word *sevenfold* appears seven times.
- The word *seventy* is used fifty-six times (7 × 8 = 56).

Notice also

- the seven churches,

- seven seals,
- seven trumpets, and
- the seven thunders—all in the book of Revelation. (See Revelation 10:1–4.)

There is also a pattern of sevens in Matthew 1:18–25, the inspired history of Christ's birth (does not include the genealogy of verses 1–17):

- The number of words in the seven-word passage is 161 (7 × 23 = 161).
- The number of vocabulary words is 77 (7 × 11 = 77).
- Six Greek words occur only in this passage and never again in Matthew. These 6 Greek words contain precisely 56 letters (7 × 8 = 56).
- There are seven distinct proper names in the passage.
- The number of Greek letters in these seven proper names is forty-two (7 × 6 = 42).
- The number of words spoken by the angel to Joseph is twenty-eight (7 × 4 = 28).

The number seven subtly permeates all of Scripture as the number of God's divine perfection and perfect order. Before his death in 1942, Ivan Panin discovered literally thousands of such mathematical patterns underlying all of the books of the Old Testament, which can be found in his book *The Inspiration of the Scriptures Scientifically Demonstrated*, where he discusses the phenomena extensively. Panin and several others examined other Hebrew literature, attempting to find such mathematical patterns, but they are not found anywhere outside the Bible. He accumulated more than forty thousand pages of detailed calculations covering most of the texts of the Bible before his death. This impressive discovery by Panin has been examined by numerous authorities, and the figures have been verified.*

Panin described his own view of Scripture after his lifelong study of it by comparing it to the limits of secular philosophy: " 'Not so, however, with The Book. For it tells of One who spake as men never spake, who was the true bread of life, that which cometh down from the heavens, of which if a man eat he shall never hunger.' He concluded with the challenge: 'My friend of the world, whose you are: Either Jesus Christ is mistaken, or you are. The answer that neither might be is only evading the issue, not settling it. But the ages have decided that Jesus Christ was not mistaken. It is for you to decide whether you shall continue to be.' "[8]

When considering the impressive details of his mathematical record, notice that a change of a single letter or word in the original languages of Hebrew or Greek would destroy the phenomenon. Then recall that Jesus insisted that the smallest letter and grammatical mark of Scripture were preserved by God: "For verily I say unto you, Till heaven and earth pass, one jot or one tittle shall in no wise pass from the law, till all be fulfilled" (Matthew 5:18, KJV).

One more aspect of that first week needs to be emphasized. On each of the first five days of the first week, God saw that everything was "good." On the sixth day, everything was declared "very good." But on the seventh day, something different happened. In the first six days, God created matter and all life. On the seventh day, He fashioned holy time. The Hebrew word *kodesh* (hallow, sanctify) first appears in the Genesis account of God creating the Sabbath. The first thing God made *holy* was not a mountain, nor a structure, nor a cave, nor a city, but time. By sanctifying Sabbath,

---

* These incredible, mathematical patterns are not limited to the number seven. There are numerous other patterns that appear in the vocabulary, grammatical forms, parts of speech, and particular forms of words. They occur throughout the whole text of the Bible, containing 31,173 verses.

Back to the Beginning

God spectacularly demonstrated His sovereignty over both space and time—over all reality—ending His creating process with this grand gesture.

With this final act, He shaped the first seven days into the first week—a unique time measurement. The weekly cycle, which God embedded in Scripture and is subsequently found around the world, is not linked to any celestial movements or cycles, as is the month to the moon's cycle, and the calendar year to our planet circling the sun. Accordingly, the seven-day weekly cycle distinguishes the Creator as sovereign over all life and *time*.

The first day of the first week found the Creator "at work" creating. But on their first full day, the newly created humans didn't work. Though given their tasks on day six (Genesis 2:15), on the seventh day, their first full day, they rested the whole day before doing any work. They rested in God's finished work. What a lesson of grace!

The German Protestant theologian Karl Barth saw this: "It is only by participation in God's celebrating that he [man] can and may and shall also celebrate on this seventh day, which is his first day. But this is just what he is commanded to do. Hence his history under the command of God really begins with the Gospel and not with the Law."[9]

And following the example of the Creator and of Adam and Eve, we can also rest each Sabbath. This blessed rest is unparalleled in any other ancient nation. The concept was revolutionary, and its implications inspired Dietrich Bonhoeffer: "In the Bible, 'rest' really means more than 'having a rest.' It means the rest after the work is accomplished, it means completion, it means the perfection and peace of God in which the world rests, it means transfiguration, it means turning our eyes absolutely upon God's being God and towards worshipping him."[10]

In the New Testament, Jesus Himself insists that the blessings of this day were intended for everyone, not just for the Jewish people, declaring that "the Sabbath was made for *man*" (Mark 2:27; emphasis added). A Jewish writer, noting the royal nature of the Sabbath day, called the Sabbath "a palace in time."[11]

Before continuing our journey through the Pentateuch, a vital interpretive point needs to be reviewed. The narratives in Genesis often proceed without mentioning how much time has elapsed between different events. In some cases, God does give major time-grounded prophecies and genealogies, yet the historical narratives are often linked together without mentioning precise periods. This is noticeable in the fifty chapters of the book of Genesis, which covers approximately 2,500 years. Contrast this with the four books Exodus, Leviticus, Numbers, and Deuteronomy, which together cover about 120 years.

It becomes obvious that there are a multitude of details and descriptions that a reader might wish for that are not recorded in the vast time of Genesis's fifty chapters. That, of course, suggests that the details that are included are all the more important! In fact, the narrator sometimes intentionally employs this method, under the inspiration of the Author of Scripture, to subtly present critical theological issues.

For example, the reader is not told how much time Adam and Eve lived in Eden before they sinned. Their sin is abruptly introduced in Genesis 3—immediately following the first two chapters describing the perfect world God created. This stark contrast serves to expose the deadly nature of sin and its results in chapter 3.

Next, Genesis 4 contains a hint of the divinely created weekly cycle when describing Cain and Abel bringing their offerings to the Lord: "Now Abel was a keeper of sheep, but Cain was a tiller of the ground. And *in the process of time* it came to pass that Cain brought an offering of the fruit of the ground to the LORD. Abel also brought of the firstborn of his flock and of their fat" (Genesis 4:2–4; emphasis added).

The opening phrase of verse 3, often translated "in the process of time," would more accurately be translated "at the end of days"—as some marginal readings rightly indicate. Of course, the phrase does indicate a passage of time. However, a careful reading of the first Genesis narratives would signal that the only "end of days" mentioned so far is the end of the first seven days with the Sabbath. Thus, the two brothers' actions "at the end of days" suggest that they were bringing their offerings on the Sabbath.

Old Testament history continues with dreadful descriptions of the impact of evil on the human race, which led to divine judgment: "Then the LORD saw that the *wickedness of man was great in the earth, and that every intent of the thoughts of his heart was only evil continually*" (Genesis 6:5; emphasis added). The previous genealogies (Genesis 5) have given a general sense of time passing, leading into Genesis 6:5, which registers the vast extent and deepening of sin's grip on humanity with superlative graphic language allowing no exceptions: "*every* intent . . . *only evil continually.*"

Genesis 6–9 describes the call of Noah, the building of the ark, the viciousness of the Flood storm, the waters then subsiding—and finally, the release from the ark of Noah, his family, and the animals. Though the Sabbath is not specifically mentioned, the weekly cycle has been indicated:

- *Genesis 7:4.* "For after *seven more days* I will cause it to rain on the earth forty days and forty nights, and I will destroy from the face of the earth all living things that I have made." God announced that judgment against vile human wickedness would commence on the seventh day.
- *Verse 10.* "And it came to pass after *seven days* that the waters of the flood were on the earth."
- *Genesis 8:10.* "And he [Noah] waited yet *another seven days*, and again he sent the dove out from the ark."
- *Verse 12.* "So he waited yet *another seven days* and sent out the dove, which did not return again to him anymore."

The weekly cycle is obviously functioning.

What is called the "patriarchal period" fills the rest of the book of Genesis. Some commentators suggest that there is no mention of the patriarchs keeping the Sabbath. There is, however, divine mention of obedience to God's law long before Sinai. For example, when God renewed the covenant with Isaac, Abraham's son:

> Then the LORD appeared to him and said: "Do not go down to Egypt; live in the land of which I shall tell you. Dwell in this land, and I will be with you and bless you; for to you and your descendants I give all these lands, and I will perform the oath which I swore to Abraham your father. And I will make your descendants multiply as the stars of heaven; I will give to your descendants all these lands; and in your seed all the nations of the earth shall be blessed; because *Abraham obeyed My voice and kept My charge, My commandments, My statutes, and My laws*" (Genesis 26:2–5; emphasis added).

When God blesses Isaac, covenant language is obvious, copying the wording of the covenant (cf. Genesis 22:16–18; Genesis 12:1–3) given to Abraham: "I will perform the oath which I swore to Abraham your father. And I will make your descendants multiply as the stars of heaven; I will give to your descendants all these lands; and in your seed all the nations of the earth shall be blessed" (verses 3, 4).

God then informs Isaac He will do this "because Abraham obeyed My voice and kept My charge, My commandments, My statutes, and My laws" (verse 5). God could have merely stated that Abraham was obedient because obedience does imply an ethical standard. However, God was very precise and declared what Abraham was obedient to: "My charge, My commandments, My statutes, and My laws" (verse 5). This is definitive language, particularly considering that the Decalogue has not been proclaimed from Mount

Sinai—and will not be for a long time yet. It is not stretching the meaning of the text to suggest that God's declaration hints that Abraham kept the Sabbath—which is found within the "commandments" to which God said Abraham was obedient.

The weekly cycle is again referred to in the narratives of Jacob when unwittingly he married Leah after working for Rachel for seven years. Jacob complains about this to his new father-in-law, and Laban responded:

> "Fulfill her *week*, and we will give you this one also for the service which you will serve with me still another seven years."
>
> Then Jacob did so and fulfilled her *week*. So he gave him his daughter Rachel as wife also (Genesis 29:27, 28; emphasis added).

This incidental mention of the week is another cue that the weekly cycle is fully operational during the patriarchal period.

The book of Exodus

Continuing our journey through the Pentateuch, we will become increasingly aware that the narratives express theology and are not merely telling a story. For example, we see the Sabbath in the book of Exodus before Sinai. In forty chapters, the book refers to it fourteen times. It is, of course, especially highlighted in the heart of the Decalogue. The fourth commandment, about the Sabbath, contains approximately one-third of all the words in the Decalogue. The commandment, however, is not the first time Sabbath is brought up.

Ellen White mentions in *Patriarchs and Prophets* that when God "commissioned" Moses to return to Egypt after forty years of shepherding, one of the first things Moses did was to restore the Sabbath. She writes, "In their bondage the Israelites had to some extent lost the knowledge of God's law, and they had departed from its precepts. The Sabbath had been generally disregarded, and the exactions of their taskmasters made its observance apparently impossible. But Moses had shown his people that obedience to God was the first condition of deliverance; and the efforts made to restore the observance of the Sabbath had come to the notice of their oppressors."[12] Exodus chapter five hints at this through the reaction of Pharaoh to the request of Moses and Aaron: "Moses and Aaron, why do you *take the people from their work?* Get back to your labor" (verse 4; emphasis added).

The Pharaoh of the Exodus was used to enforcing slave labor seven days a week. After Moses restored the Sabbath upon his arrival in Egypt, the Egyptian ruler had apparently gotten wind that his Israelite slaves were not cooperating one day a week. He clarified his frustration even further with his second statement: "And Pharaoh said, 'Look, the people of the land are many now, and *you make them rest from their labor!*' " (verse 5; emphasis added). The word for "rest" that the Egyptian ruler used reveals he was even aware of the name of the Israelite's "day off." It is built on the root of the Hebrew word *shabbat.*

After the Israelites escaped Egypt, the Sabbath is again in the spotlight. Before the Israelites arrived at Mount Sinai, where the Decalogue was spoken to them by God, He spoke about the Sabbath and His law! As the freed slaves journeyed to the Promised Land, one of the many miracles bestowed on them by Yahweh was the gift of manna for their meals. "Then the LORD said to Moses, 'Behold, I will rain bread from heaven for you. And the people shall go out and gather a certain quota every day, that I may *test them*, whether they will walk in *My law* or not. And it shall be on the sixth day that they shall prepare what they bring in, and it shall be twice as much as they gather daily' " (Exodus 16:4, 5; emphasis added).

The people were given instructions concerning the collecting of manna for six days—and told how they could rest on the seventh day by gathering a double portion of it on Friday. Moses explained

Back to the Beginning

God's command regarding the Sabbath: "This is what the LORD has said: 'Tomorrow is *a Sabbath rest, a holy Sabbath to the LORD*' " (verse 23; emphasis added). Apparently, some did not have enough faith or deliberately chose to ignore the directives for "it happened that some of the people went out on the seventh day to gather, but they found none" (verse 27). The divine response is striking. " 'How long do you refuse to keep *My commandments and My laws*? See! For the LORD has given you the Sabbath; therefore He gives you on the sixth day bread for two days. Let every man remain in his place; let no man go out of his place on the seventh day.' So the people rested on the seventh day" (verses 28–30; emphasis added).

The Israelites hadn't even experienced the dramatic divine presentation of the Decalogue on Mount Sinai—yet God asks how long they are going to refuse to keep His commandments and laws! Keeping the Sabbath was a test of believing God even before Sinai—a test found more than once in the Bible, as we will see.

For the next forty years of wilderness wanderings, God miraculously continued to mark off each week and each Sabbath with manna meals. Note the multiple miracles involved:

- On the first five days of the week, everyone could gather what they needed, but any left over would spoil.
- On the sixth day, a double amount could be gathered for each person, and when it was saved for the next day, it didn't spoil.
- There was no manna to gather on the seventh day, the Sabbath, and the people could rest.
- This weekly cycle was divinely marked for forty years.

The psalmist later described these miracle manna meals as heavenly food!

He had commanded the clouds above,

And opened the doors of heaven,
Had rained down manna on them to eat,
And given them of *the bread of heaven*.
Men ate *angels' food*;
He sent them food to the full (Psalm 78:23–25; emphasis
added).

The Israelites finally arrived at Mount Sinai—and what happened
there truly was an utterly unique occasion in all human history.
God called Moses up the mountain and described His desire for
His people: " 'You have seen what I did to the Egyptians, and
how I bore you on eagles' wings and brought you to Myself. Now
therefore, if you will indeed obey My voice and keep My covenant,
then you shall be a special treasure to Me above all people; for all
the earth is Mine. And you shall be to Me a kingdom of priests
and a holy nation.' These are the words which you shall speak to
the children of Israel" (Exodus 19:4–6).

This is a remarkable introduction to the presentation of the law.
The Great Lawgiver doesn't come across as a tyrant, demanding
obedience or else. Rather, He wanted the Israelites to think of Him
like a mother eagle carrying her children on her wings, wanting
to teach her eaglets how to fly. God used this warm analogy to
describe bringing the released slaves, not to a court setting, but to
Himself: "I bore you on eagles' wings and *brought you to Myself.*"

In His instructions to the former slaves—and subsequently to
us—God includes the gift of resting for one-seventh of our lives!
No other god ever offered such a gift. The ancient Near Eastern
origin accounts speak of the gods creating humans so that they
could work for them. Yes, God commanded work for six days—yet
He intended even that work to be a blessing just as His own work
of creating had been for Him.

He also described His dream of the Israelites being His special
treasure—all of them a kingdom of priests and a holy nation.

Back to the Beginning

These are not the words of a potentate trying to force obedience through a massive load of restrictions. These are the commands of God, the Liberator, who wants His redeemed people to stay free! The Exodus first and *then* the giving of the law—this sequence is significant! The psalmists clearly grasped this and composed hymns in praise of the law: "Oh, how I love Your law! It is my meditation all the day" (Psalm 119:97).

However, when the freed slaves arrived at Mount Sinai, no one could casually enter the presence of the holy God. Three days of preparation were needed.

> Then it came to pass on the third day, in the morning, that there were thunderings and lightnings, and a thick cloud on the mountain; and the sound of the trumpet was very loud, so that all the people who were in the camp trembled. And Moses brought the people out of the camp to meet with God, and they stood at the foot of the mountain. Now Mount Sinai was completely in smoke, because the LORD descended upon it in fire. Its smoke ascended like the smoke of a furnace, and the whole mountain quaked greatly. And when the blast of the trumpet sounded long and became louder and louder, Moses spoke, and God answered him by voice (Exodus 19:16–19).

Moses would often remind the freed slaves of the nature of their divine deliverance. He recalled the extraordinary nature of the awesome Sinai event in his farewell message to Israel:

> "For what great nation is there that has God so near to it, as the LORD our God is to us, for whatever reason we may call upon Him? And what great nation is there that has such statutes and righteous judgments as are in all this law which I set before you this day? Only take heed to yourself, and diligently keep yourself, lest you forget the things your eyes

have seen, and lest they depart from your heart all the days of your life. And teach them to your children and your grand-children, especially concerning the day you stood before the LORD your God in Horeb, when the LORD said to me, 'Gather the people to Me, and I will let them hear My words, that they may learn to fear Me all the days they live on the earth, and that they may teach their children.'

"Then you came near and stood at the foot of the mountain, and the mountain burned with fire to the midst of heaven, with darkness, cloud, and thick darkness. And the LORD spoke to you out of the midst of the fire. You heard the sound of the words, but saw no form; you only heard a voice. So He declared to you His covenant which He commanded you to perform, the Ten Commandments; and He wrote them on two tablets of stone. . . .

". . . But the LORD has taken you and brought you out of the iron furnace, out of Egypt, to be His people, an inheritance, as you are this day" (Deuteronomy 4:7–13, 20).

The Decalogue—the "Ten Words," as the Hebrew Bible consistently refers to them—is the towering ethical document in Scripture. It is quoted by almost every biblical writer following the Exodus, whether psalmists, prophets, or historians. In the New Testament, Jesus Himself refers to the Decalogue, affirming its eternal nature. The apostle Paul likewise speaks of the far-reaching claims of God's law, often directly quoting it in his various letters and epistles. The great apostle's cross-cultural ministry to the Gentiles finds him instructing new Christians on how the law's boundaries extend to the deeply hidden secrets of the human heart, searching thoughts and motives—because the curse of sin is such deep contamination. The canon closes with the book of Revelation and its significant reference to "those who keep the commandments" (Revelation 14:12).[13]

Back to the Beginning

Because the giving of the law at Sinai was so overwhelming, some have thought that the divine law was a new ethical system given especially to the Jewish people. However, Decalogue precepts weren't new at Sinai. They were already the standard of right and wrong in the Genesis narratives. Note a few examples:

- The "tree of knowledge of good and evil" implies an ethical standard (Genesis 2:16, 17).
- When God confronted Cain about murdering his brother, Cain did not plead innocence—that he didn't know murder was wrong—he only complained about his punishment (Genesis 4).
- Along with the mention of the weekly cycle, Abraham's obedience to God's law is commended by God throughout the Abrahamic narratives.
- Jacob told his family to put away their idols before they returned to Bethel. This shows the importance long before Sinai of rejecting idolatry (Genesis 35:1–3).
- Two different pagan kings scold Abraham, and then Isaac, for lying about who their wives were, which almost led to adultery (Genesis 20; 26)—even pagan kings knew adultery was wrong—though Abraham (cf. Genesis 20:1–6) and Isaac (Cf. Genesis 26:8–10) had lied to them.
- Coveting, lying, stealing, and murder happened as a result of Dinah's rape (Genesis 34) because her brothers knew that *such a thing ought not to be done* (verse 7, RSV; emphasis added).
- Joseph refused adultery with his boss's wife, telling the pagan woman that adultery would be a sin not just against her husband but especially against God (Genesis 39).

Returning our attention to Sinai, we see that the fourth commandment of the Decalogue is rich with Sabbath theology.

Rediscovering the Glory the Sabbath

The unique treasure of its blessed twenty-four hours can be seen from several angles:

- It is the divine Creator's personal setting apart of holy time.
- It is His chosen day of rest—not any of the other six days.
- God had already set the example back in Eden.
- He commands it on Sinai with His own voice.
- He wrote it twice in stone, not trusting its permanent copying to any human writer—though He had Moses write down the civil and ritual laws.
- The fourth commandment, regarding the Sabbath, is the longest in the Decalogue—and found at its heart.
- None of the Jewish feasts were commanded in the Decalogue.
- The stone tablets of the divinely engraved Decalogue were placed inside the sacred ark, under the mercy seat, in the Most Holy Place of the sanctuary.
- The Mosaic laws were stored outside of the sacred ark.
- The Sabbath was given in Eden before sin; all other feasts were given after sin.
- The Sabbath is celebrated weekly, but the feast days, yearly.

The first word of the fourth commandment, "Remember" (*zahkar*), occurs eight times in the book of Exodus—always in the context of God's covenant with Israel (Exodus 2:24; 3:15; 6:5; 13:3; 20:8, 24; 23:13; 32:13). And all eight times connect two specific memorial days in salvation history: the seventh-day Sabbath from Creation (Exodus 20:8) and the day of the Exodus (Exodus 13:3). Other similarities of these two grand memorial days include mention that both are based on the seven-day cycle: the Sabbath on Creation week and the Passover and Feast of Unleavened Bread observed for seven days.

The meaning of the first word of the fourth commandment,

remember, involves more than just knowing the right day, though that is, of course, included. The primary meaning is "to call to mind" or "to give thought to."[14] This would involve an active "appreciation and commitment"[15] toward the Lord and His covenant. And in this case, both the Sabbath and the entire Decalogue form the basis of Israel's covenant with Yahweh.

The commandment to remember the Sabbath was never meant to be an arbitrary constraint. It was meant to bring refreshment, not restriction. This is obvious in the equality of the seven beneficiaries of the Decalogue's "manifesto of freedom": "In it you shall do no work: you, nor your son, nor your daughter, nor your male servant, nor your female servant, nor your cattle, nor your stranger who is within your gates" (Exodus 20:10). Even female servants and animals are included in its blessings. This was unheard of in the ancient Near East and in many places still today.

When Moses reiterated this inclusive and gracious statute, he mentioned the included persons and also the land's sabbatical: "Six years you shall sow your land and gather in its produce, but the seventh year you shall let it rest and lie fallow, that *the poor* of your people may eat; and what they leave, *the beasts of the field* may eat. In like manner you shall do with your vineyard and your olive grove. Six days you shall do your work, and on the seventh day you shall rest, that *your ox and your donkey may rest, and the son of your female servant and the stranger may be refreshed*" (Exodus 23:10–12; emphasis added).

The muscular wording of the Decalogue causes some to flinch from its supposed sternness rather than recognizing its blessings. However, the Lawgiver's introductory words, often excluded or ignored, give an entirely different flavor to the Decalogue. These words should be allowed to undergird any study of the Decalogue: "And God spoke all these words, saying: 'I am the Lord your God, who brought you out of the land of Egypt, out of the house of bondage' " (Exodus 20:1, 2).

Many modern English translations designate these opening divine words as the "prologue" to the Decalogue. However, Jewish tradition rightly attests that these opening divine words are really part of the first commandment. And when included that way, the "prologue" puts an entirely different flavor on all Ten Commandments, including the fourth one about the Sabbath. Those opening words make all ten precepts a gift of grace!

God first delivered the enslaved Israelites—and only *after* He saved them did He speak to them the "Ten Words" from Sinai! Therefore, keeping the Sabbath, or any of the commandments, is not a requirement to receive grace. Rather, these "Ten Words" are the bond or seal to keep God's people secure in the redemption already received! The Lawgiver didn't demand the keeping of the Sabbath so that His people could be saved. The Sabbath was a weekly sign of His grace! The sequence in the Exodus chapters is clear:

- First, any Israelites or Egyptians who chose could be spared the judgment of the final deadly plague by being "under the blood" of the Passover lamb.
- *Then* came deliverance from slavery.
- Finally, at Sinai, God spoke His law and established His covenant with His people, telling them through Moses: "Thus you shall say to the children of Israel: 'You have seen that I have talked with you from heaven. . . . In every place where I record My name I will come to you, and I will bless you' " (Exodus 20:22–24).

The commandments forbade lying, stealing, killing, and committing adultery. However, the Sabbath continued to invite people to fellowship with the Creator on the day He set apart as holy—His sign, in time, of His gracious desire to be with His people just as it had been at Creation. The fourth commandment regarding the Sabbath still retains its awesome central function.

At Sinai, the Great Lawgiver included the reason for the importance of the seventh day by referring back to the original institution of the Sabbath during Creation week, repeating the three identical verbs used in Genesis 2:1–3—"rested," "blessed," "hallowed." If a person accepts the Sinai commandment, the Creation record must also be accepted. Among other things, the Sabbath strikes directly against modern evolutionary thinking. The fourth commandment, pointing to the divine Creation of this world, indicates that life is not here on earth by chance. Nor is it still continuing to evolve through millions of years—for God "finished" His work (Genesis 2:1–3).

All through Scripture, this foundational assertion is repeated. For example, in the worship scene in heaven found in the book of Revelation, God is praised as Creator:

Whenever the living creatures give glory and honor and thanks to Him who sits on the throne, who lives forever and ever, the twenty-four elders fall down before Him who sits on the throne and worship Him who lives forever and ever, and cast their crowns before the throne, saying:

"You are worthy, O Lord,
To receive glory and honor and power;
For You created all things,
And by Your will they exist and were created" (Revelation 4:9–11; emphasis added).

The Sabbath commandment states God's right as Creator to command, and also human ability to conform, for humans were created in God's image. Thus, the Decalogue, when rightly understood, is not a constrictive force against us. The law expresses the true nature of human beings. Keeping it is not an outward mechanical exercise but a reflection of an intensely personal relationship with the Creator. And our weekly calendars will reflect our values!

What is more, God's law also reminds us of His grace and mercy toward us, following sin's tragic and deadly corruption. Sin drastically and fundamentally corrupted human nature, as we saw in the earlier Genesis narratives. However, the law is not designed to keep us in line—it is intended to restore us. No wonder the psalmist joyfully exclaimed: "O, how I love Your law! It is my meditation all the day" (Psalm 119:97). Ellen White wrote elegantly about the positive nature of God's law:

> The ten holy precepts spoken by Christ upon Sinai's mount were the revelation of the character of God, and made known to the world the fact that He had jurisdiction over the whole human heritage. That law of ten precepts of the greatest love that can be presented to man is the voice of God from heaven speaking to the soul in promise. "This do, and you will not come under the dominion and control of Satan." There is not a negative in that law, although it may appear thus. It is DO, and Live. . . . The Lord has given His holy commandments to be a wall of protection around His created beings.[16]

The scope of the fourth commandment alone is vast. We must allow it to remind us that we are not "earning" salvation by keeping it. God saved us first. We can be declared righteous only by accepting salvation. "Remembering" the Sabbath is the sign that God is making us holy as the prophet Ezekiel declared, quoting God's promise:

> "For I will take you from among the nations, gather you out of all countries, and bring you into your own land. Then I will sprinkle clean water on you, and you shall be clean; *I*

will cleanse you from all your filthiness and from all your idols. I will give you a new heart and put a new spirit within you; I will take the heart of stone out of your flesh and give you a heart of flesh. I will put My Spirit within you and cause you to walk in My statutes, and you will keep My judgments and do them. Then you shall dwell in the land that I gave to your fathers; you shall be My people, and I will be your God" (Ezekiel 36:24–28; emphasis added).

We need the Sabbath as a continual reminder of our divine creation and sustained existence. The apostle Paul insisted to the Roman Christians that there is no excuse not to believe in the Creator because all nature testifies about Him:

For the wrath of God is revealed from heaven against all ungodliness and unrighteousness of men, who suppress the truth in unrighteousness, because what may be known of God is manifest in them, for God has shown it to them. *For since the creation of the world His invisible attributes are clearly seen, being understood by the things that are made, even His eternal power and Godhead*, so that they are without excuse, because, although they knew God, they did not glorify Him as God, nor were thankful, but became futile in their thoughts, and their foolish hearts were darkened. Professing to be wise, they became fools, and changed the glory of the incorruptible God into an image made like corruptible man—and birds and four-footed animals and creeping things (Romans 1:18–23; emphasis added; he was reflecting the sentiments of the ancient psalmist in Psalm 14:1).

Exodus also instructs that the Creator never intended the seventh-day Sabbath to be a restriction or a burden, but a day of rejoicing with the Creator. It reminds us that He wants to bless every person: "And the LORD spoke to Moses, saying, 'Speak also to the children of Israel, saying: "Surely My Sabbaths you shall keep, for *it is a sign* between Me and you throughout your generations, that you may know that I am the LORD who sanctifies you" ' " (Exodus 31:12, 13; emphasis added).

The Sabbath carries a heavy weight of sacred meaning about both Creation and Redemption. It must be guarded against distortion by mere external conformity. We don't make the Sabbath holy, nor is it kept by our works. Rather, the Sabbath links us in fellowship with the Creator—reminding that we belong to God two ways: through Creation and Redemption.

It also reminds us that the Creator is a beneficent God, guarding His people against overwork: "Six days you shall work, but on the seventh day you shall rest; in plowing time and in harvest you shall rest" (Exodus 34:21). Divine grace again becomes apparent—He commands Sabbath rest even during plowing and harvest time when the weather would be a vital factor in successful farming.

The emperor Constantine, in his edict of AD 321, was not so considerate: "Constantine, Emperor Augustus, to Helpidius: On the venerable day of the sun let the magistrates and people residing in cities rest, and let all workshops be closed. In the country, however, persons engaged in agriculture may freely and lawfully continue their pursuits, because it often happens that another day is not as suitable for grain sowing or for vine planting; lest by neglecting the proper moment for such operations the bounty of heaven should be lost."[17]

The great Creator wants His people to realize that He is the reason for the harvest and that He can be trusted with it while allowing us to rest each Sabbath.

Some are troubled by the narrative about the Sabbath in Exodus 35: "Then Moses gathered all the congregation of the children of Israel together, and said to them, 'These are the words which the LORD has commanded you to do: Work shall be done for six days, but the seventh day shall be a holy day for you, a Sabbath of rest to the LORD. Whoever does any work on it shall be put to death. You shall kindle no fire throughout your dwellings on the Sabbath day' " (verses 1–3).

It is argued that the death penalty for gathering wood on the Sabbath is too harsh. However, one needs to recall when reading this narrative in the book of Exodus that Moses elaborated on God's directives for intentional, unintentional, and presumptuous sins and their penalties in the book of Numbers (Numbers 15:22–36). Laws for Israel were framed within the Old Testament theocracy, and defiant, deliberate sins were rightly taken very seriously. Numbers 15 records one incident when the death sentence for breaking the Sabbath was administered:

> Now while the children of Israel were in the wilderness, they found a man gathering sticks on the Sabbath day. And those who found him gathering sticks brought him to Moses and Aaron, and to all the congregation. They put him under guard, because it had not been explained what should be done to him.
>
> Then the LORD said to Moses, "The man must surely be put to death; all the congregation shall stone him with stones outside the camp." So, as the LORD commanded Moses, all the congregation brought him outside the camp and stoned him with stones, and he died (verses 32–36).

It is instructive to note that this incident is found in the section of Numbers 15 that deals with intentional, defiant sins. In this case, it infers that the Sabbath breaking was deliberate rebellion. Abraham Heschel describes the covenantal relationship between God and His people in terms of a divine pathos—that God's involvement in human history is never impersonal. God is not a distant spectator watching the events of history from afar. He "is personally and emotionally involved in the life of man."[18] Moreover, this section in Numbers 15 follows immediately after the verses in the chapter dealing with unintentional sins—bringing out the critical difference between the two types of sins.

Ellen White's commentary on this situation is also helpful in pointing out the issues involved:

The mixed multitude that came up with the Israelites from Egypt were a source of continual temptation and trouble. They professed to have renounced idolatry and to worship the true God; but their early education and training had molded their habits and character, and they were more or less corrupted with idolatry and with irreverence for God. *They were oftenest the ones to stir up strife and were the first to complain, and they leavened the camp with their idolatrous practices and their murmurings against God.*

Soon after the return into the wilderness, an instance of Sabbath violation occurred, under circumstances that rendered it a case of peculiar guilt. The Lord's announcement that He would disinherit Israel had roused a spirit of rebellion. One of the people, angry at being excluded from Canaan, and determined to show his defiance of God's law, ventured upon the open transgression of the fourth commandment by going out to gather sticks upon the Sabbath. During the sojourn in the wilderness the kindling of fires upon the seventh day had been strictly prohibited. The prohibition was not to extend to the land of Canaan, where the severity of the climate would often render fires a necessity; but *in the wilderness, fire was not needed for warmth. The act of this man was a willful and deliberate violation of the fourth commandment—a sin, not of thoughtlessness or ignorance, but of presumption.*

He was taken in the act and brought before Moses. It had already been declared that Sabbathbreaking should be punished with death, but it had not yet been revealed how the penalty was to be inflicted. The case was brought by Moses before the Lord, and the direction was given, "The man shall be surely put to death: all the congregation shall stone him with stones without the camp." Numbers 15:35. *The sins of blasphemy and willful Sabbathbreaking received the same punishment, being equally an expression of contempt for the authority of God.*[19]

The book of Leviticus

The twenty-seven chapters of the book of Leviticus are of an entirely different literary nature than the narratives in Genesis and Exodus. Rather than historical records, this book deals with the religious and civil laws given to Israel by their Redeemer.

In these laws are fourteen sections concerned with the Sabbath. There are also six references to the Sabbath being kept by the land in chapters 25 and 26. Sabbath rest remains all-encompassing: for humans, animals, and the land itself.

Leviticus 19:3 links the Sabbath with family ties—reflecting the same connection as in the Decalogue. The fourth commandment about the Sabbath, and fifth commandment regarding family relationships, are the only two stated in the positive sense: "Remember the Sabbath day" and "Honor your father and mother." The other eight commandments begin with, "you shall not."

In Leviticus 19:30, the Sabbath is linked with the sanctuary: "You shall keep My Sabbaths and reverence My sanctuary: I am the LORD."

Leviticus 23 teaches us that the Sabbath is also a time given for worship. The structure and wording of the chapter make this clear. Verses 1–3 speak of the weekly Sabbath:

And the LORD spoke to Moses, saying, "Speak to the children of Israel, and say to them: 'The feasts of the LORD, which you shall proclaim to be holy convocations, these are My feasts.

" 'Six days shall work be done, but the seventh day is a Sabbath of solemn rest, a holy convocation. You shall do no work on it; it is the Sabbath of the LORD in all your dwellings.' "

A "convocation" refers to public worship gatherings.

The deity then continues describing, in order, the yearly festivals beginning with the spring festivals:

- Passover and Feast of Unleavened Bread (verses 4–8). This is the first feast of the Israelite ritual calendar.
- Feast of First Fruits (verses 9–14).
- Feast of Weeks (verses 15–22).

These are the fall festivals:

- Feast of Trumpets (verses 23–25).
- The Day of Atonement (verses 26–32).
- Feast of Tabernacles (verses 33–36).

God then separates the yearly festivals and the weekly Sabbath once more: "These are the feasts of the LORD which you shall proclaim to be holy convocations, to offer an offering made by fire to the LORD, a burnt offering and a grain offering, a sacrifice and drink offerings, everything on its day—*besides the Sabbaths of the LORD*, besides your gifts, besides all your vows, and besides all your freewill offerings which you give to the LORD" (verses 37, 38; emphasis added).

The great Creator called His people to celebrate His goodness. The calendar of the yearly feasts kept His calendar of salvation history before His people. Additionally, each week, the seventh day was set apart to ground His people in His goodness, His holiness, and the joy and privilege of worshiping Him as a result of knowing Him.

Back to the Beginning

We still need time to worship. It can be easily crowded out of our busy modern work schedules and lifestyles. But every seventh day, we are invited to take time to re-center our lives in the Creator by worshiping Him. We can hurry around day after day doing good things and being good, but this will not save us. We talk about grace and think we understand it, yet we still rely on our own efforts—forgetting that we cannot save ourselves. Sabbath gives us the time to focus on the Creator's divine grace, which *will* save us! "For by grace you have been saved through faith, and that not of yourselves; it is the gift of God, not of works, lest anyone should boast. For *we are His workmanship, created in Christ Jesus for good works, which God prepared beforehand that we should walk in them*" (Ephesians 2:8–10; emphasis added).

Leviticus 24 follows the sanctuary ritual: "And you shall take fine flour and bake twelve cakes with it. Two-tenths of an ephah shall be in each cake. You shall set them in two rows, six in a row, on the pure gold table before the Lord. And you shall put pure frankincense on each row, that it may be on the bread for a memorial, an offering made by fire to the Lord. Every Sabbath he shall set it in order before the Lord continually, being taken from the children of Israel by an everlasting covenant" (verses 5–8). Fresh bread on the Sabbath! What wonderful symbolism!

Leviticus 25 speaks of the Sabbath "years" and the Jubilee. In the first seven verses, the sabbatical for the land is discussed, reminding again that the Sabbath is intended to be an all-encompassing blessing for people, including male servants, female servants, and visiting strangers, for the animals, and even for the soil:

And the Lord spoke to Moses on Mount Sinai, saying, "Speak to the children of Israel, and say to them: 'When you come into the land which I give you, then the land shall keep a sabbath to the Lord. Six years you shall sow your field, and six years you shall prune your vineyard, and gather its fruit;

but in the seventh year there shall be a sabbath of solemn rest for the land, a sabbath to the Lord. You shall neither sow your field nor prune your vineyard. What grows of its own accord of your harvest you shall not reap, nor gather the grapes of your untended vine, for it is a year of rest for the land. And the sabbath produce of the land shall be food for you: for you, your male and female servants, your hired man, and the stranger who dwells with you, for your livestock and the beasts that are in your land—all its produce shall be for food' " (verses 1–7).

The parameters are vast—and ever gracious! Here again, the blessings are specific, including male and female servants, hired employees, and guests—and also the hardworking animals! Offering rest to farm animals is not found in any other ancient tradition, nor is the soil ever granted rest. God makes it clear that He cares about all creation!

Immediately following this gracious gift of rest for an entire year comes the grandest sabbatical gift of the jubilee year. The year of jubilee is described in great detail, significantly counting by sevens:

"And you shall count seven sabbaths of years for yourself, seven times seven years; and the time of the seven sabbaths of years shall be to you forty-nine years. Then you shall cause the trumpet of the Jubilee to sound on the tenth day of the seventh month; on the Day of Atonement you shall make the trumpet to sound throughout all your land. And you shall consecrate the fiftieth year, and proclaim liberty throughout all the land to all its inhabitants. It shall be a Jubilee for you; and each of you shall return to his possession, and each of you shall return to his family. That fiftieth year shall be a Jubilee to you; in it you shall neither sow nor reap what grows of its own accord, nor gather the grapes of your untended vine.

For it is the Jubilee; it shall be holy to you; you shall eat its produce from the field.

"In this Year of Jubilee, each of you shall return to his possession. And if you sell anything to your neighbor or buy from your neighbor's hand, you shall not oppress one another. According to the number of years after the Jubilee you shall buy from your neighbor, and according to the number of years of crops he shall sell to you. According to the multitude of years you shall increase its price, and according to the fewer number of years you shall diminish its price; for he sells to you according to the number of the years of the crops. Therefore you shall not oppress one another, but you shall fear your God; for I am the LORD your God" (verses 8–17).

Liberty is the main theme—liberty from all debts and oppression occurring from debts owed and from the hard work of cultivation and harvesting. The enormous graciousness of the sabbath gift is again highlighted.

Leviticus 26 spells out the covenant blessings and curses with covenant language: "I will walk among you and be your God" (verse 12).

In verses 1 and 2, the Sabbath is connected to the first two commandments of the Decalogue, showing that the Decalogue is a complete system with each commandment closely aligned with the others:

"You shall not make idols for yourselves;
neither a carved image nor a sacred pillar shall you rear up
  for yourselves;
nor shall you set up an engraved stone in your land, to bow
  down to it;
for I am the LORD your God.

Rediscovering the Glory the Sabbath

You shall keep My Sabbaths and reverence My sanctuary:
I am the LORD."

As in Leviticus 19:30, the Sabbath is also linked with the sanctuary.

This chapter then presents the many blessings that obedience would bring; rain, abundant harvests of both tree and ground crops, peace among all the nations surrounding them, and the Israelites would be fruitful and multiply. God would walk among them and be their God, and they would be His people, confirming His covenant with them (Leviticus 26:9, 12). He concluded by reminding them of the salvation He had already bestowed on them: "I am the LORD your God, who brought you out of the land of Egypt, that you should not be their slaves; I have broken the bands of your yoke and made you walk upright" (verse 13).

If that wasn't motivation enough to stay in covenant relationship with their Redeemer, God spelled out the dire consequences of forsaking Him and the covenant with nine verses of covenant curses.

"But if you do not obey Me, and do not observe all these
commandments,
and if you despise My statutes, or if your soul abhors My
judgments, so that you do not perform all My commandments, but break My covenant,
I also will do this to you:
I will even appoint terror over you, wasting disease and fever
which shall consume the eyes and cause sorrow of heart.
And you shall sow your seed in vain, for your enemies shall
eat it.
I will set My face against you, and you shall be defeated by
your enemies. Those who hate you shall reign over you,
and you shall flee when no one pursues you.

"And after all this, if you do not obey Me, then I will punish
you seven times more for your sins. . . .

"And after all this, if you do not obey Me, but walk contrary
to Me,
then I also will walk contrary to you in fury;
and I, even I, will chastise you seven times for your sins"
(verses 14–28).

Later in chapter 26, the importance of the sabbatical for the land
is repeated. Verse 34 closes the curses with a beautiful promise:
God described how He would use the Israelites' future (deserved)
Babylon exile to grant the land it's neglected rest:

"I will scatter you among the nations and draw out a sword
after you;
your land shall be desolate and your cities waste.
Then the land shall enjoy its sabbaths as long as it lies desolate
and you are in your enemies' land;
then *the land shall rest and enjoy its sabbaths.*
As long as it lies desolate it shall rest—
for the time it did not rest on your sabbaths when you dwelt
in it" (verses 33–35; emphasis added).

Twice God mentions the land enjoying its sabbaths—another
hint of the Creator's affection for what He created!

Because the Israelites did not carry out the gracious divine stipulations for themselves, their community, their animals, and the
land, God had to move in and give the soil its rest. Tragically, the
later historian recorded the Israelites' unfaithfulness with their
many abominations—fulfilling what Jeremiah predicted for many
years would happen. The people were taken captive to Babylon,
and their temple was burned. This fulfilled "the word of the LORD

by the mouth of Jeremiah, *until the land had enjoyed her Sabbaths. As long as she lay desolate she kept Sabbath,* to fulfill seventy years" (2 Chronicles 36:21; emphasis added).

Throughout all these catastrophes, God remained faithful, never forsaking His people. They broke the covenant, but God never did.

Why was God so insistent on Sabbath rest? Is He a legalist? Are His commandments, including the Sabbath commandment, truly a gift? God never enslaves anyone. Nor are His commands given to manipulate obedience. No, God redeems and delivers first, then provides the guidelines to guard that freedom. He wants His ransomed children to stay free as He continues His work of redemption.

Notice how Moses reminded Israel of this: "And Moses called all Israel, and said to them: 'Hear, O Israel, the statutes and judgments which I speak in your hearing today, that you may learn them and be careful to observe them. *The LORD our God made a covenant with us in Horeb.* The LORD did not make this covenant with our fathers, but *with us, those who are here today, all of us who are alive*' " (Deuteronomy 5:1–3; emphasis added).

It is easy to overlook the striking nature of Moses' words. The people of the original generation of the Exodus had (except for Caleb, Joshua, and Moses) perished in the forty years of wandering in the wilderness because of their defiant sinfulness. But Moses insisted that God made the covenant with all of them present there *that day,* thus, instructing that the covenant is always a present reality!

The Sabbath teaching in Exodus and Leviticus is a record that the Sabbath is a pure gift and benefit. It is not a restrictive demand or burden. Nor is it a task we must accomplish. Rather, it is a guide enabling us to stay in the grace already received. God is not enslaving nor placing a heavy yoke on us. Instead, He wants to secure us in His vast redeeming plans. The psalmist understood this as he described the inauguration of the priesthood for the newly constructed desert sanctuary:

> Behold, how good and how pleasant it is
> For brethren to dwell together in unity!
>
> It is like the precious oil upon the head,
> Running down on the beard,
> The beard of Aaron,
> Running down on the edge of his garments.
> It is like the dew of Hermon,
> Descending upon the mountains of Zion;
> *For there the* LORD *commanded the blessing—*
> Life forevermore (Psalm 133; emphasis added).

God commands blessings! "The ten holy precepts spoken by Christ upon Sinai's mount . . . made known to the world the fact that He had jurisdiction over the whole human heritage. That law of ten precepts of the greatest love that can be presented to man is the voice of God from heaven speaking to the soul in promise, 'This do, and you will not come under the dominion and control of Satan.' There is not a negative in that law, although it may appear thus. It is DO, and Live."[20]

The book of Numbers
The book of Numbers, detailing the sanctuary furniture and services, along with a few narratives of wilderness wanderings, mentions the Sabbath in three sections. Describing the Sabbath offerings, the reader is reminded that the Sabbath was not intended to be twenty-four hours of total inactivity. A special sacrifice, in addition to the daily sacrifice, was to be offered on the Sabbath day (Numbers 28:9, 10).

The book of Deuteronomy

In the final book of the Pentateuch, Moses gives his farewell address to the Israelites. He speaks about the Decalogue and recites the commandments. As he reiterates the "Ten Words" (Deuteronomy 5), he also discusses their far-reaching nature, just as later Jesus would do in His sermon on the mount. In fact, chapters 12–26 have been shown not to be a random collection of wisdom sentiments. They are a structured, extended commentary explicating the wide parameters of each commandment. Stephen Kaufman and others have shown that these chapters explain the sequence and content of the Decalogue stipulations, arranged "with consummate literary artistry."[21] Kaufman substantiates the sequence and arrangement this way:

Commandment	Deuteronomy passage	Description
1, 2	12:1–31	Worship
3	13:1–14:27	Name of God
4	14:28–16:17	Sabbath
5	16:18–18:22	Authority
6	19:1–22:8	Homicide
7	22:9–23:19	Adultery
8	23:20–24:7	Theft
9	24:8–25:4	False charges
10	25:5–16	Coveting

Some critics have tried to discredit the slight variation of the wording of the fourth commandment in Deuteronomy. However, Moses elaborates on the vast parameters of the Sabbath command by mentioning the redemption of Israel from slavery rather than Creation week as a reason to keep the Sabbath. He thereby connects two divine Creation events—the Creation of the world and the creation of His people. Both times the divine Creation fashioned something out of nothing. Both events emphasize the mighty power of the great God!

The section dealing with the Sabbath commandment also includes how the poor are to be treated. This is not an odd, one-time connection with the Sabbath, however. Later, God through Isaiah describes faulty Sabbath keeping because the poor are being neglected:

"If you take away the yoke from your midst,
The pointing of the finger, and speaking wickedness,
If you extend your soul to the hungry
And satisfy the afflicted soul,
Then your light shall dawn in the darkness,
And your darkness shall be as the noonday.
The Lord will guide you continually,
And satisfy your soul in drought,
And strengthen your bones;
You shall be like a watered garden,
And like a spring of water, whose waters do not fail.
Those from among you
Shall build the old waste places;
You shall raise up the foundations of many generations;
And you shall be called the Repairer of the Breach,
The Restorer of Streets to Dwell In.

"If you turn away your foot from the Sabbath,
From doing your pleasure on My holy day,
And call the Sabbath a delight,
The holy day of the Lord honorable,
And shall honor Him, not doing your own ways,
Nor finding your own pleasure,
Nor speaking your own words,

Rediscovering the Glory the Sabbath

Then you shall delight yourself in the LORD;
And I will cause you to ride on the high hills of the earth,
And feed you with the heritage of Jacob your father.
The mouth of the LORD has spoken" (Isaiah 58:9–14).

1. Norman Wirzba, *Food and Faith: A Theology of Eating* (New York: Cambridge University Press, 2011), 183, 184.

2. Ellen G. White, "The Love of God. How Manifested," *Union Conference Record*, June 1, 1900, 4.

3. Ellen G. White, "The Creation Sabbath," *Signs of the Times*, February 28, 1884.

4. Ellen G. White, *Manuscript Releases*, vol. 1 (Silver Spring, MD: Ellen G. White Estate, 1981), 160, 161.

5. Ellen G. White, "The Test of Loyalty," *Signs of the Times*, February 13, 1896; emphasis added.

6. Jiří Moskala, "The Sabbath in the First Creation Account," *Journal of the Adventist Theological Society* 13, no. 1 (Spring 2002): 57.

7. The following section is heavily indebted to and adapted from Grant R. Jeffrey, "The Astonishing Pattern of SEVENS in Genesis 1:1," in *The Signature of God: Astonishing Bible Codes* (Frontier Research Publications, Inc., 1996).

8. Jeffrey, 230–237.

9. Karl Barth, *Church Dogmatics*, vol. 3, pt. 4 (New York: T&T Clark, 2004), 52.

10. Dietrich Bonhoeffer, *Creation and Fall: A Theological Interpretation of Genesis 1–3* (New York: Macmillan, 1959), 40.

11. Abraham Joshua Heschel, *The Sabbath: Its Meaning for Modern Man* (New York: Farrar, Straus and Giroux, 1951), 12.

12. Ellen G. White, *Patriarchs and Prophets* (Mountain View, CA: Pacific Press®, 1958), 258.

13. Jo Ann Davidson, "The Decalogue Predates Mount Sinai: Indicators from the Book of Genesis," *Journal of the Adventist Theological Society* 19, no. 1, 2 (2008): 61–81.

14. A. Bowling, "*zakar*," in *The Hebrew and Aramaic Lexicon of the Old Testament*, ed. R. L. Harris, G. L. Archer, and B. K. Waltke, vol. 1 (Chicago: Moody Press, 1980), 241.

15. L. C. Allen, "*zkr*," in *New International Dictionary of the Old Testament Theology and Exegesis*, ed. W. A. VanGemeren, vol. 4 (Grand Rapids, MI: Eerdmanns, 1980), 68.

16. Ellen G. White, *Sons and Daughters of God* (Washington, DC: Review and Herald®, 1955), 53.

17. Tamara Cohn Eskenazi, Daniel J. Harrington, and William H. Shea, *The Sabbath in Jewish and Christian Traditions* (New York: Crossroad, 1991), 246.

18. Abraham J. Heschel, *The Prophets* (New York: Harper and Row, 2001), 298.

19. Ellen G. White, *Patriarchs and Prophets* (Mountain View, CA: Pacific Press®, 1958), 408, 409; emphasis added.

20. Ellen G. White, *The Faith I Live By* (Washington, DC: Review and Herald®, 1958), 95.

Back to the Beginning

21. Stephen A. Kaufman, "The Structure of the Deuteronomic Law," *Maarav* 1, no. 2 (Spring 1979): 105–158, quotation on page 125. That Deuteronomy12–25 represent sequential explanations of the Decalogue was seen in principle as early as Philo of Alexander and also understood by Protestant Reformers Luther and Calvin. But Kaufman presents a more systematic discussion, taking cues from other ancient Near East law codes.

Chapter Two

The Sabbath in
Old Testament History and Song

The Historical Books are called the Former Prophets in the
Hebrew tradition,* which highly exalts their content as more
than just a collection of historical events. Again, as in all Hebrew
narrative writing, the historical details imply and inform theology.
The fourth commandment is not quoted in the historical books,
but the Sabbath is embedded and implied.

In 2 Kings, the narrative of the Shunammite woman contains
an incidental mention of the Sabbath. One of the residents of
Shunem, "a notable woman" (2 Kings 4:8), a hospitable person,
noticed that the prophet Elisha occasionally traveled through the
town and would invite him in for a meal. She and her husband
then built a "guest room" for the traveling prophet's comfort.

When Elisha wanted to express some "tangible" gratitude, his
servant noted that the woman and her husband had no children.
Elisha then assured her that within the next year, she would have
a son, and she did. One day, the child suffered some kind of
heatstroke and was rushed to his mother. Though she cared for
him "till noon" (verse 20), the little lad died.

This is where the incidental mention of the Sabbath enters the
narrative. The mother then urged her husband: "Please send me

_____

* What are called the Major Prophets in the Christian tradition are called the Later
Prophets in the Hebrew Bible. What are called the Minor Prophets in the Christian
tradition are called the Book of the Twelve in the Hebrew Bible.

one of the young men and one of the donkeys, that I may run to the man of God and come back." He responded, "Why are you going to him today? It is neither the New Moon nor the Sabbath" (verses 22, 23).

This brief notation instructs that the Sabbath was still being kept—and that somehow the prophets were involved in the worship tradition.

The books of First and Second Chronicles, also part of the Historical Books (or Former Prophets), include several references to the Sabbath.

The duties of the Levites for the Sabbath day are recorded in 1 Chronicles 23:

So when David was old and full of days, he made his son Solomon king over Israel.

And he gathered together all the leaders of Israel, with the priests and the Levites. Now the Levites were numbered from the age of thirty years and above; and the number of individual males was thirty-eight thousand. Of these, twenty-four thousand were to look after the work of the house of the LORD, six thousand were officers and judges, four thousand were gatekeepers, and *four thousand praised the LORD with musical instruments, "which I made," said David, "for giving praise."*

Also David separated them into divisions among the sons of Levi: Gershon, Kohath, and Merari. . . .

The Levites were . . . *to stand every morning to thank and praise the LORD, and likewise at evening; and at every presentation of a burnt offering to the LORD on the Sabbaths* and on the New Moons and on the set feasts, by number *according to the ordinance governing them*, regularly before the LORD; and that they should attend to the needs of the tabernacle of meeting, the needs of the holy place, and the needs of the sons of Aaron their brethren in the work of the house of the Lord (1 Chronicles 23:1–6, 27–32; emphasis added).

"Giving praise" was a "required duty"! The Sabbath has continued and is seen to be a day for praise—with a Levitical choir of four thousand no less!

When Solomon was gathering supplies to build the temple, his letter to the king of Tyre requesting needed materials and workmen included mention of the Sabbath in the context of extolling such a Great God:

Then Solomon sent to Hiram king of Tyre, saying:

> As you have dealt with David my father, and sent him cedars to build himself a house to dwell in, so deal with me. Behold, I am building a temple for the name of the Lord my God, to dedicate it to Him, to burn before Him sweet incense, for the continual showbread, for the burnt offerings morning and evening, on *the Sabbaths*, on the New Moons, and on the set feasts of the Lord our God. This is an ordinance forever to Israel.
>
> And the temple which I build will be great, for our God is greater than all gods. But who is able to build Him a temple, since heaven and the heaven of heavens cannot contain Him? Who am I then, that I should build Him a temple, except to burn sacrifice before Him? (2 Chronicles 2:3–6; emphasis added).

Sabbath is mentioned again in the record of Solomon's reverence for the Sabbath as the services for the new temple begin:

Then Solomon offered burnt offerings to the Lord on the altar of the Lord which he had built before the vestibule, according to the daily rate, offering according to the commandment of Moses, for *the Sabbaths*, the New Moons, and the three appointed yearly feasts—the Feast of Unleavened Bread, the Feast of Weeks, and the Feast of Tabernacles. And, according to the order of David his father, he appointed the divisions of the priests for their service, the Levites for their duties (to praise and serve before the priests) as the duty of each day required, and the gatekeepers by their divisions at each gate; for so David the man of God had commanded. They did not depart from the command of the king to the priests and Levites concerning any matter or concerning the treasuries.

Now all the work of Solomon was well-ordered from the day of the foundation of the house of the LORD until it was finished. So the house of the LORD was completed (2 Chronicles 8:12–16; emphasis added).

Later, wicked Queen Athaliah unlawfully ascended the throne of Judah by deliberately murdering all her relatives. However, the wife of the high priest was able to hide baby Joash and spare his life: "And he was hidden with them in the house of God for six years, while Athaliah reigned over the land" (2 Chronicles 22:12).

After six years of the violent, cruel rule of Queen Athaliah, the high priest Jehoida "strengthened himself, and made a covenant with the captains of hundreds" (2 Chronicles 23:1) to terminate the unlawful, wicked rule of Athaliah:

Then all the assembly made a covenant with the king in the house of God. And he said to them, "Behold, the king's son shall reign, as the LORD has said of the sons of David. This is what you shall do: *One-third of you entering on the Sabbath, of the priests and the Levites*, shall be keeping watch over the doors; one-third shall be at the king's house; and one-third at the Gate of the Foundation. All the people shall be in the courts of the house of the LORD. But let no one come into the house of the LORD except the priests and those of the Levites who serve. They may go in, for they are holy; but all the people shall keep the watch of the LORD. And the Levites shall surround the king on all sides, every man with his weapons in his hand; and whoever comes into the house, let him be put to death. You are to be with the king when he comes in and when he goes out."

So the Levites and all Judah did according to all that Jehoiada the priest commanded. And each man took his men *who were to be on duty on the Sabbath, with those who were going off duty on the Sabbath*; for Jehoiada the priest had not dismissed the divisions. And Jehoiada the priest gave to the captains of hundreds the spears and the large and small shields which had belonged to King David, that were in the temple of God. Then he set all the people, every man with his weapon in his hand, from the right side of the temple to the left side of the temple, along by the altar and by the temple, all around the king. And they brought out the king's son, put the crown on him, gave him the Testimony, and made him king. Then Jehoiada and his sons anointed him, and said, "Long live the king!" (verses 3–11; emphasis added).

When Athaliah heard the great celebration with musicians and singers, she came to investigate. Seeing the newly crowned king, she tore her royal robes, yelling, "Treason, treason." However, Jehoida had planned carefully, and armed men were ready to carry out his commands. That Sabbath became a day of judgment against evil—just as it had earlier when on "the seventh day" divine judgment was administered to the condemned city of Jericho (see Joshua 6:15–18).

After Athaliah's judgment, Jehoida called the people to renew their covenant with God by destroying the sites of Baal-worship apostasy, and restoring true worship:

> Then Jehoiada made a covenant between himself, the people, and the king, that they should be the LORD's people. And all the people went to the temple of Baal, and tore it down. They broke in pieces its altars and images, and killed Mattan the priest of Baal before the altars. Also Jehoiada appointed the oversight of the house of the LORD to the hand of the priests, the Levites, whom David had assigned in the house of the LORD, to offer the burnt offerings of the LORD, as it is *written in the Law of Moses*, with rejoicing and with singing, as it was established by David (2 Chronicles 23:16–18; emphasis added).

Disregarding the comprehensive parameters of the biblical Sabbath was a major aspect of bringing to close the tragic history of the Israelites' unfaithfulness and apostasy because they deliberately refused to give up idol worship. The dreadful results of this refusal impacted all facets of life because Baal worship was corrupt and violent. The chronicler recorded many tragic details of Israel being taken captive to Babylon. In conclusion, however, he mentioned one positive particular—that the land could finally be blessed when Israel was deported. Only an all-powerful Creator could bring blessing out of such a terrible apostasy: "And those who escaped from the sword he [Nebuchadnezzar] carried away to Babylon, where they became servants to him and his sons until the rule of the kingdom of Persia, to fulfill the word of the LORD by the mouth of Jeremiah, *until the land had enjoyed her Sabbaths. As long as she lay desolate she kept Sabbath, to fulfill seventy years*" (2 Chronicles 36:20, 21; emphasis added).

This again brings to mind how Sabbath blessings are meant to surround all family members, the servants (male and female), the animals, and even the soil! Apparently, Israel had not been faithful in granting the soil its sabbatical blessings. But during the seventy years of captivity, God reversed that.

The Psalter

The psalter opens proclaiming the joy found in keeping God's law:

> Blessed is the man
> Who walks not in the counsel of the ungodly,
> Nor stands in the path of sinners,
> Nor sits in the seat of the scornful;
> But *his delight is in the law of the* LORD,
> And in His law he meditates day and night (Psalm 1:1, 2;
>   emphasis added).

The longest book in the Bible has a unique connection to the Sabbath. Since the psalms were what we would call the Old Testament "hymnbook" for worship, it is not surprising to find mentions of the Sabbath sprinkled all through the 150 "chapters." For example, the phrase "works of Your hands" is a dominant theme found in many of the "hymns." The psalmists are constrained to praise God when considering the wonders of the created world. Moreover, singing these hymns on the Sabbath, the worshipers would be rejoicing in the glories of Creation week, which climaxed on the seventh-day Sabbath.

Nature is sometimes referred to as God's "second book." However, the glories of creation are much older than the Written Word! More accurately, the biblical canon should be called God's "second book"—and the created world His first! The psalms often draw attention to it. Psalm 8 is one of many:

> O LORD, our LORD,
> How excellent is Your name in all the earth,
> Who have set Your glory above the heavens!

Out of the mouth of babes and nursing infants
You have ordained strength,
Because of Your enemies,
That You may silence the enemy and the avenger.

When I consider Your heavens, the work of Your fingers,
The moon and the stars, which You have ordained,
What is man that You are mindful of him,
And the son of man that You visit him?
For You have made him a little lower than the angels,
And You have crowned him with glory and honor (verses 1–5).

Though it doesn't cite in detail all that was created that first week, the things mentioned make clear that the psalmist was expressing admiration over the entire created world. Bible writers often do this, citing a few details that suggest the whole picture. For example, in the New Testament, the apostle Paul will refer to one or two of the commandments. He was not demonstrating a forgetful mind that could remember only a few. Nor is Paul singling out one or two commandments as the only important ones. Rather, in this way, he refers to the entire Decalogue. We will review those passages later.

Psalm 19 is another psalm that refers to creation. Verses 1–6 describe the glories of the heavens, and especially the sun, which presents powerful and convincing testimony about the almighty Creator—for no corner of the universe is unreached by such an overwhelming witness. Paul makes this same analogy to the Romans: "For since the creation of the world His invisible attributes are clearly seen, being understood by the things that are made, even His eternal power and Godhead, so that they are without excuse" (Romans 1:20).

Verses 7–13, following immediately, create an analogy by connecting God's "two books." The glory of God's Word is compared to the magnificent nature of the sun—its circuit being as far-reaching. As God is the Creator of the heavens, the sun, and the cycle of day and night, which grants life, so His Word also creates life. And of course, the Sabbath, being the climax of Creation week, would be exalted in this reference to creation. "To discern the unity between 19:1–6 and 19:7 is to begin to appreciate the psalmist's daring claim and the psalms' radical implications."[1]

Psalm 24 begins by naming the Creator:

The earth is the LORD's, and all its fullness,
The world and those who dwell therein.
For He has founded it upon the seas,
And established it upon the waters (verses 1, 2).

Next follows a description of the life of the worshiper by mentioning a couple of the commandments—this, of course, implying the entire Decalogue, including the fourth commandment.

The chorus in verses 7–10 praises the "King of glory." He was introduced as the Creator at the beginning of the psalm. Now, He is presented as a mighty Warrior. Ellen White asserts that this chorus is what the angels sang as they escorted Jesus back to heaven after His resurrection:

All heaven was waiting the hour of triumph when Jesus should ascend to His Father. Angels came to receive the King of glory and to escort Him triumphantly to heaven. After Jesus had blessed His disciples, He was parted from them and taken up. And as He led the way upward, the multitude of captives who were raised at His resurrection followed. A multitude of the heavenly host were in attendance, while in heaven an innumerable company of angels awaited His coming. As they ascended to the Holy City, the angels who escorted Jesus cried out, "Lift up your heads, O ye gates; and be ye lifted up, ye everlasting doors; and the King of glory shall come in." The angels in the city cried out with rapture, "Who is this King of glory?" The escorting angels answered in triumph, "The Lord strong and mighty, the Lord mighty in battle! Lift up your heads, O ye gates; even lift them up, ye everlasting doors; and the King of glory shall come in!" Again the waiting angels asked, "Who is this King of glory?" and the escorting angels answered in melodious strains, "The Lord of hosts, He is the King of glory." And the heavenly train passed into the city of God. Then all the heavenly host surrounded their majestic Commander, and with the deepest adoration bowed before Him and cast their glittering crowns at His feet. And then they touched their golden harps, and in sweet, melodious strains filled all heaven with rich music and songs to the Lamb who was slain, yet lives again in majesty and glory.[2]

Psalm 33 is also filled with adoration for the Creator and amazement for all He created:

Rejoice in the LORD, O you righteous!
For praise from the upright is beautiful.
Praise the LORD with the harp;
Make melody to Him with an instrument of ten strings.
Sing to Him a new song;
Play skillfully with a shout of joy.

For the word of the LORD is right,
And all His work is done in truth.
He loves righteousness and justice;
The earth is full of the goodness of the LORD.

By the word of the LORD the heavens were made,
And all the host of them by the breath of His mouth.

He gathers the waters of the sea together as a heap;
He lays up the deep in storehouses.

Let all the earth fear the LORD;
Let all the inhabitants of the world stand in awe of Him.
For He spoke, and it was done;
He commanded, and it stood fast.

The LORD brings the counsel of the nations to nothing;
He makes the plans of the peoples of no effect.
The counsel of the LORD stands forever,
The plans of His heart to all generations.
Blessed is the nation whose God is the LORD,
The people He has chosen as His own inheritance.

The LORD looks from heaven;
He sees all the sons of men.
From the place of His dwelling He looks
On all the inhabitants of the earth;
He fashions their hearts individually;
He considers all their works (verses 1–15).

Based on what God has done, the psalmist expressed confidence in the Creator's promise of salvation: "For the word of the LORD is right, and all His work is done in truth" (verse 4). Of course, it goes without mention that the creation of the Sabbath is implied, as only the Creator can touch time and create a week. And Sabbath gives occasion for singing this praise song in worship. In fact, Creation psalms often led to doxology. These verses of poetic praise are no careless interruptions but rather an expressive culmination of Old Testament theology!

Psalm 104 is an extensive commentary on the seven-day Creation week. Each section spotlights a day of Creation week, sometimes connecting the creative action with its blessed results. Only now, the verbs are in the present tense! This results in an impressive "hymn" celebrating that the Creator is not some distant landlord but presently upholding and sustaining His creation:

- Verses 1, 2, day one: light

  Bless the Lord, O my soul!

  O Lord my God, You are very great:
  You are clothed with honor and majesty,
  Who cover Yourself with light as with a garment,
  Who stretch out the heavens like a curtain.

- Verses 3, 4, day two: separation of firmament and water

  He lays the beams of His upper chambers in the waters,
  Who makes the clouds His chariot,
  Who walks on the wings of the wind,
  Who makes His angels spirits,
  His ministers a flame of fire.

- Verses 5–18, day three: dry land, grass, and trees to provide food

  You who laid the foundations of the earth,
  So that it should not be moved forever,
  You covered it with the deep as with a garment;
  The waters stood above the mountains.
  At Your rebuke they fled;
  At the voice of Your thunder they hastened away.
  They went up over the mountains;
  They went down into the valleys,
  To the place which You founded for them.

Rediscovering the Glory the Sabbath

You have set a boundary that they may not pass over,
That they may not return to cover the earth.

He sends the springs into the valleys;
They flow among the hills.
They give drink to every beast of the field;
The wild donkeys quench their thirst.
By them the birds of the heavens have their home;
They sing among the branches.
He waters the hills from His upper chambers;
The earth is satisfied with the fruit of Your works.

He causes the grass to grow for the cattle,
And vegetation for the service of man,
That he may bring forth food from the earth,
And wine that makes glad the heart of man,
Oil to make his face shine,
And bread which strengthens man's heart.
The trees of the LORD are full of sap,
The cedars of Lebanon which He planted,
Where the birds make their nests;
The stork has her home in the fir trees.
The high hills are for the wild goats;
The cliffs are a refuge for the rock badgers.

- Verses 19–23, day four: sun and moon

He appointed the moon for seasons;
The sun knows its going down.
You make darkness, and it is night,
In which all the beasts of the forest creep about.
The young lions roar after their prey,
And seek their food from God.

When the sun rises, they gather together
And lie down in their dens.
Man goes out to his work
And to his labor until the evening.

• Verses 24–30, days five and six: living creatures

O Lord, how manifold are Your works!
In wisdom You have made them all.
The earth is full of Your possessions—
This great and wide sea,
In which are innumerable teeming things,
Living things both small and great.
There the ships sail about;
There is that Leviathan
Which You have made to play there.

These all wait for You,
That You may give them their food in due season.
What You give them they gather in;
You open Your hand, they are filled with good.
You hide Your face, they are troubled;
You take away their breath, they die and return to their dust.
You send forth Your Spirit, they are created;
And You renew the face of the earth.

• Verses 31–35, day seven: the Sabbath

May the glory of the Lord endure forever;
May the Lord rejoice in His works.
He looks on the earth, and it trembles;
He touches the hills, and they smoke.

I will sing to the LORD as long as I live;
I will sing praise to my God while I have my being.
May my meditation be sweet to Him;
I will be glad in the LORD.
May sinners be consumed from the earth,
And the wicked be no more.

Bless the LORD, O my soul!
Praise the LORD!

The psalm opens and concludes with the psalmist's adoration. An attitude of praise for all of the creation can't be helped! And the final section about the seventh day again instructs us that the Sabbath is not a restrictive straitjacket but a day that calls forth high praise for the Creator!

Psalm 136 praises God for His two mighty acts: Creation (verses 1–9) and redemption (of Old Testament Israel) from Egypt (verses 10–26). So impressive are these creative acts of God that the refrain "For His mercy endures forever" is repeated after each detail is mentioned!

Moses had already connected these two great divine redemptive acts. First, in his Exodus record, he presented God pronouncing the Decalogue on Sinai, with the fourth commandment detailing God's mighty power during Creation week. Then, in Deuteronomy 5, in his farewell "sermon," Moses cited God's mighty Exodus redemptive power in the fourth commandment. This is not a contradiction, as some scholars try to claim, but rather it depict God's awesome creative power both during Creation week and during the Exodus: both times He was creating something from nothing, as we saw earlier.

Psalm 92 deserves special attention because it is a song dedicated exclusively to the Sabbath—and is still presently sung in Jewish worship on Sabbath. The word *Sabbath* is only found in the ancient title "A Psalm. A Song for the Sabbath day."* However, a pattern of sevens can be seen within its verses. Only Psalm 92, among the 150 psalms, extensively highlights the number seven, providing internal evidence that the writer was highlighting the Sabbath:

- It is the only psalm in the entire psalter where the divine name *Yahweh* is repeated seven times.
- It describes seven positive qualities for the righteous and seven different epithets for the wicked.
- The midpoint and climax of the psalm (verse 8) is flanked by seven verses (1–7 and 9–15).
- The overall structure contains five strophes, or stanzas, each with six lines, except for the climactic middle stanza, which contains seven lines.

The fifteen lofty verses are arranged in an elegant chiastic structure, which also accentuates the richness of the Sabbath, highlighting the central motivation for Sabbath observance in the middle verse.†

Exultation: A
Verses 1–3 (6 lines)
God's character

Creation: B
Verses 4–6 (6 lines)
God's creative works

---

* All the earliest Hebrew manuscripts (such as the Dead Sea Scrolls) and other ancient versions (e.g., LXX) contain this superscription. In New Testament times, God's people accepted the headings of the Psalms as authentic. For example, Jesus Himself based His final clinching argument for His Messiahship upon the validity and reliability of the superscription in the Psalms.

† See Richard Davidson's notes on Psalm 92 in the *Andrews Study Bible* (Berrien Springs, MI: Andrews University Press, 2010), 745.

Redemption: C
Verse 7 (3 lines)
God's work in the past

Culmination: D
Verse 8 (1 line)

Redemption: C1
Verse 9 (3 lines)
God's work in the future

Sanctification: B1
Verses 10–12 (6 lines)
God's re-creative work

Glorification: A1
Verses 13–15 (6 lines)
God's character

This type of elegant literary chiastic structure can be found all through the Old Testament. Such patterns aid in interpretation, opening rich veins of understanding. In the case of Psalm 92, it lavishly exalts the royal nature of the Sabbath.

The inaugural three verses first suggest the mood for the Sabbath. This reminds us that rituals, traditions, and customs are not enough. Rather, each person is instructed that everything about Sabbath worship should flow from a rejoicing heart! The motive for Sabbath joy is a living relationship with the Lord of the Sabbath, the Creator!

The next three verses (4–6) recall God's creative power. The Hebrew phrase "Your deeds" often appears in connection with God's mighty acts throughout history (Psalms 44:1; 64:9; 90:16; 111:3; 143:5), with the phrase "the works of Your hands" most often referring to God's mighty works as Creator—which caused all heaven to rejoice! God Himself described this to Job:

"Where were you when I laid the foundations of the earth?
Tell Me, if you have understanding.
Who determined its measurements?
Surely you know!
Or who stretched the line upon it?
To what were its foundations fastened?
Or who laid its cornerstone,
When the morning stars sang together,
And all the sons of God shouted for joy?" (Job 38:4–7; emphasis added).

The central three verses of Psalm 92 (7–9), link the psalm to God's redemption of His people in the prime Old Testament example of His miraculous deliverance of Israel from centuries of slavery in Egypt. The passage is structured in the same way as Moses' recitation of the Sabbath commandment in Deuteronomy. (Jesus also underscored the close relationship between Creation and salvation by announcing His ministry of redemption on the Sabbath [Luke 4:16–21], as we will study later.)

Verses 10–12 portray sanctification. The parameters of the Sabbath blessing include the divine promise of redemption from sin. Both Exodus 31:13 and later Ezekiel 20:12 recall this profound blessing of the Sabbath as a sign of sanctification: "I also gave them My Sabbaths, to be a sign between them and Me, that they might know that I am the LORD who sanctifies them" (verse 12).

Psalm 92 concludes with the glorious promise of glorification! A literal translation of verse 13 reads, "*transplanted* into the house of the LORD, they will flourish in the courts of our God." The Hebrew word translated "transplanted" is a technical term referring to the eschatological entrance into heaven. There, it is promised, we will still bring forth fruit in old age and ever be "full of sap and green" (verse 14, RSV)—anticipating being glorified with the Sabbath celebrating that magnificent future. Thereby the Sabbath links us from our beginnings in Eden to Eden restored. The Reformer John Calvin grasped this when he wrote: "The Lord through the seventh day has sketched for His people the coming perfection of His Sabbath in the last day."[3]

A modern Jewish scholar also insists that the contents of this psalm describe and correspond to the major biblical themes of the Sabbath.[4] Another Jewish writer encourages: "The Sabbath is the inspirer; the others days the inspired."[5] Ellen White also linked her Sabbath theology to Psalm 92:

All things were created by the Son of God. "In the beginning was the Word, and the Word was with God. . . . All things were made by Him; and without Him was not anything made that was made." John 1:1–3. And since the Sabbath is a memorial of the work of creation, it is a token of the love and power of Christ.

The Sabbath calls our thoughts to nature, and brings us into communion with the Creator. In the song of the bird, the sighing of the trees, and the music of the sea, we still may hear His voice who talked with Adam in Eden in the cool of the day. And as we behold His power in nature we find comfort, for the word that created all things is that which speaks life to the soul. He "who commanded the light to shine out of darkness, hath shined in our hearts, to give the light of the knowledge of the glory of God in the face of Jesus Christ." 2 Corinthians 4:6.

It was this thought that awoke the song,—

"Thou, Lord, hast made me glad through Thy work;
I will triumph in the works of Thy hands.

74

The Sabbath in Old Testament History and Song

O Lord, how great are Thy works!
And Thy thoughts are very deep."
Psalm 92:4, 5.[6]

The prophets

The prophets consistently and regularly reminded the Israelites that Yahweh urged a distinct social reality affecting every area of life. Sinful forms of oppression, lawlessness, and violence were to be addressed and dealt with. Old Testament prophets always connected serving Yahweh with both private and public life. Decalogue stipulations were never relaxed. And the Sabbath figures in extensively as part of Israel's apostasy.

Of all the Ten Commandments, only in one of them does God command remembrance. He declares specifically, "Remember"— the verb in the imperative form. This underscores that Sabbath keeping is important. In urging His people to remember, Yahweh insists that what He sets forth is of great importance and must never be forgotten. Apparently, there is nothing worse than forgetting the Sabbath, nor anything more dangerous to separate us from Him. Forgetting Sabbath makes it easier to forget the great Creator God. And this personal call to remember implies that hearts are involved. Remembering the Sabbath involves much more than the cessation of physical labor to take a nap.

There is no commandment in the Decalogue of which God speaks more solemnly or that is commended more diligently by the prophets. Nor is there any other commandment about which Deity raises greater legal complaints and reproaches against those who violate it. For example, when He brings charges against the ingratitude of His people and their despising of His law, the thing He mentions most often is that they violated and desecrated the Sabbath. And, when He calls people back into fellowship, the foremost thing He commands them is the observance of this day—as though all of the law was founded on and included in this one commandment. Moses had also communicated Yahweh's sentiment about the Sabbath:

> "Speak also to the children of Israel, saying: 'Surely My Sabbaths you shall keep, for it is a sign between Me and you throughout your generations, that you may know that I am the LORD who sanctifies you. You shall keep the Sabbath, therefore, for it is holy to you. Everyone who profanes it shall surely be put to death; for whoever does any work on it, that person shall be cut off from among his people. Work shall be done for six days, but the seventh is the Sabbath of rest, holy to the LORD. Whoever does any work on the Sabbath day, he shall surely be put to death. Therefore the children of Israel shall keep the Sabbath, to observe the Sabbath throughout their generations as a perpetual covenant. It is a sign between Me and the children of Israel forever; for in six days the LORD made the heavens and the earth, and on the seventh day He rested and was refreshed' " (Exodus 31:13–17).

There is never any accusation in the Old Testament that Israel is worshiping on the wrong day. The people are accused, however, of losing their connection with God even though diligently maintaining an exemplary outward show. Even worse, they were convinced that external conformity was enough. They wanted to keep up the external facade—convinced that God is only concerned about outward acts and not worried about the state of the heart.

During the preexilic years, morality and genuine religion were at a low ebb. Worship had deteriorated so much that God was repulsed with Israel's externalism. Isaiah, Jeremiah, Hosea, and Amos all record critical and negative attitudes of Sabbath keeping.

Isaiah
Isaiah spoke on three major points regarding Sabbath:

- chapter 56, the inclusive nature of the Sabbath
- chapter 58, the definition of true Sabbath keeping
- chapter 66, the assurance that the Sabbath is eternal

The book of Isaiah opens with God's lengthy accusation against His Sabbath-keeping people:

Hear, O heavens, and give ear, O earth!
For the LORD has spoken:
"I have nourished and brought up children,
And they have rebelled against Me;
The ox knows its owner
And the donkey its master's crib;
But Israel does not know,
My people do not consider" (Isaiah 1:2, 3).

In the indictment of these verses, God is saying: "You have fallen below the level of animals. Even animals know their master. But you don't know Me. If you don't want to know Me, why bother with all the rituals? They are worthless by themselves. I am not interested in external formalities. I want your heart." He continues:

Alas, sinful nation,
A people laden with iniquity,
A brood of evildoers,
Children who are corrupters!
They have forsaken the LORD,
They have provoked to anger
The Holy One of Israel,
They have turned away backward (verse 4).

Unless the Lord of hosts
Had left to us a very small remnant,

Rediscovering the Glory the Sabbath

We would have become like Sodom,
We would have been made like Gomorrah.

Hear the word of the LORD,
You rulers of Sodom;
Give ear to the law of our God,
You people of Gomorrah:
"To what purpose is the multitude of your sacrifices to Me?"
Says the LORD.
"I have had enough of burnt offerings of rams
And the fat of fed cattle.
I do not delight in the blood of bulls,
Or of lambs or goats.

"When you come to appear before Me,
Who has required this from your hand,
To trample My courts?
Bring no more futile sacrifices;
Incense is an abomination to Me.
The New Moons, *the Sabbaths, and the calling of assemblies—*
I cannot endure iniquity and the sacred meeting.
Your New Moons and your appointed feasts
My soul hates;
They are a trouble to Me,
I am weary of bearing them.
When you spread out your hands,
I will hide My eyes from you;
Even though you make many prayers,
I will not hear.
Your hands are full of blood.

"Wash yourselves, make yourselves clean;
Put away the evil of your doings from before My eyes.

Cease to do evil,
Learn to do good;
Seek justice,
Rebuke the oppressor;
Defend the fatherless,
Plead for the widow" (verses 9–17; emphasis added).

God was weary of their lifeless forms of worship and thus, through Isaiah, gave His people a lengthy litany of serious moral accusations. They were condemned for their apparently faultless ritual observances, which were used to try to mask their sinful hearts. The same thing had happened with Cain's offering in Genesis 4. It revealed his sinful heart and was not accepted by God as Ellen White comments,

Cain came before God with murmuring and infidelity in his heart in regard to the promised sacrifice and the necessity of the sacrificial offerings. His gift expressed no penitence for sin. He felt, as many now feel, that it would be an acknowledgment of weakness to follow the exact plan marked out by God, of trusting his salvation wholly to the atonement of the promised Saviour. He chose the course of self-dependence. He would come in his own merits. He would not bring the lamb, and mingle its blood with his offering, but would present his fruits, the products of his labor. He presented his offering as a favor done to God, through which he expected to secure the divine approval. Cain obeyed in building an altar, obeyed in bringing a sacrifice; but he rendered only a partial obedience. The essential part, the recognition of the need of a Redeemer, was left out.

So far as birth and religious instruction were concerned, these brothers were equal. Both were sinners, and both acknowledged the claims of God to reverence and worship. To outward appearance their religion was the same up to a certain point, but beyond this the difference between the two was great.[7]

Rediscovering the Glory the Sabbath

The prophet Isaiah underscores the centrality of the Sabbath in chapters 56–59. He shows that the Sabbath was not given just to the Jews but was intended for all peoples, including non-Jewish foreigners and even eunuchs:

Thus says the LORD:

> "Keep justice, and do righteousness,
> For My salvation is about to come,
> And My righteousness to be revealed.
> Blessed is the man who does this,
> And the son of man who lays hold on it;
> Who keeps from defiling the Sabbath,
> And keeps his hand from doing any evil."
>
> Do not let the son of the foreigner
> Who has joined himself to the LORD
> Speak, saying,
> "The LORD has utterly separated me from His people";
> Nor let the eunuch say,
> "Here I am, a dry tree."
> For thus says the LORD:
> "To the eunuchs who keep My Sabbaths,
> And choose what pleases Me,
> And hold fast My covenant,
> Even to them I will give in My house
> And within My walls a place and a name
> Better than that of sons and daughters;
> I will give them an everlasting name
> That shall not be cut off" (Isaiah 56:1–5).

All through Scripture, the moral life is linked to the Decalogue, and the Sabbath is connected to the covenant. The Sabbath is the testing truth of covenant connection just as it was in the wilderness wanderings of the released slaves and mixed multitude in Exodus 16, as we reviewed earlier:

Then the LORD said to Moses, "Behold, I will rain bread from heaven for you. And the people shall go out and gather a certain quota every day, *that I may test them, whether they will walk in My law or not.*" . . .

. . . And the LORD said to Moses, "How long do you refuse to keep My commandments and My laws? See! For the LORD has given you the Sabbath; therefore He gives you on the sixth day bread for two days. Let every man remain in his place; let no man go out of his place on the seventh day." So the people rested on the seventh day (Exodus 16:4, 28–30; emphasis added).

Recall that this happened before Sinai. According to divine messages through Isaiah, it has always been God's will that people be liberated from sin so they can enjoy a morally shaped life to its fullest.

Isaiah 58 also connects the Sabbath with social justice. The first twelve verses list social actions that Israel was guilty of neglecting, with verses 13 and 14 then leading right into the Sabbath:

"If you take away the yoke from your midst,
The pointing of the finger, and speaking wickedness,
If you extend your soul to the hungry
And satisfy the afflicted soul,
Then your light shall dawn in the darkness,
And your darkness shall be as the noonday.
The LORD will guide you continually,
And satisfy your soul in drought,
And strengthen your bones;

You shall be like a watered garden,
And like a spring of water, whose waters do not fail.
Those from among you
Shall build the old waste places;
You shall raise up the foundations of many generations;
And you shall be called the Repairer of the Breach,
The Restorer of Streets to Dwell In" (verses 9–12).

This description is immediately connected to the Sabbath:

"If you turn away your foot from the Sabbath,
From doing your pleasure on My holy day,
And call the Sabbath a delight,
The holy day of the LORD honorable,
And shall honor Him, not doing your own ways,
Nor finding your own pleasure,
Nor speaking your own words,
Then you shall delight yourself in the LORD;
And I will cause you to ride on the high hills of the earth,
And feed you with the heritage of Jacob your father.
The mouth of the LORD has spoken" (verses 13, 14).

God was seeking to remind His people that the Sabbath was to be a *delight*! And a cause for delighting in the Lord! Rightly interpreting the word "pleasure" is critical here. Its usage earlier in the chapter (verse 3) makes it clear that the Old Testament Sabbath keepers were guilty of wrongful moral treatment of others—their employees were specifically mentioned. And, even though they were worshiping on the right day, these Sabbath keepers felt no guilt in what they were doing socially, thinking they were blame-free because of their external conformity to the Decalogue.

God reprimands them for this faulty attitude, telling them that true delight comes from a heart linked to His through the

Sabbath—the day for delighting in Him. The Creator knows what will bring His children, created in His image, the highest joy—serving others as He does. This leads to true delight in Him. The Sabbath becomes a day to praise Him for His great mercy and constant care. And these become the motivation behind how others are treated. This passage in Isaiah also provides another important Old Testament proof that Israel was to be a light to the Gentiles.

Jeremiah

Jeremiah was another prophetic voice. Called while still a youth, he was assured by God that his youth would be no hindrance to his calling:

Then the word of the LORD came to me, saying:

"Before I formed you in the womb I knew you;
Before you were born I sanctified you;
I ordained you a prophet to the nations."

Then said I:

"Ah, Lord GOD!
Behold, I cannot speak, for I am a youth."

But the LORD said to me:

"Do not say, 'I am a youth,'
For you shall go to all to whom I send you,
And whatever I command you, you shall speak.
Do not be afraid of their faces,
For I am with you to deliver you," says the LORD (Jeremiah 1:4–8).

Jeremiah then served forty years through the reign of five kings—a long and difficult time of extreme apostasy during which the people denied anything was wrong. Jeremiah began prophesying before Daniel, long calling for a genuine spiritual revival. Daniel was taken to Babylon and remained God's mouthpiece. During the terrible sieges of Jerusalem, God addressed His wayward people through Jeremiah:

" 'You shall call Me, "My Father,"
And not turn away from Me.'
Surely, as a wife treacherously departs from her husband,
So have you dealt treacherously with Me,
O house of Israel," says the LORD.

A voice was heard on the desolate heights,
Weeping and supplications of the children of Israel.
For they have perverted their way;
They have forgotten the LORD their God.

"Return, you backsliding children,
And I will heal your backslidings" (Jeremiah 3:19–22).

More than any of the other prophets, Jeremiah called Israel's attention to the counsels in the book of Deuteronomy. He emphasized the Mosaic law and how obedience would bring the highest blessing to every heart. However, extreme disobedience was the discouraging response from the people:

Thus says the LORD:

"Stand in the ways and see,
And ask for the old paths, where the good way is,
And walk in it;

Then you will find rest for your souls.
But they said, 'We will not walk in it' " (Jeremiah 6:16).

Jeremiah endeavored to avert the threatened destruction of Jerusalem. Faithfully calling for repentance, he was labeled a traitor and severely punished. Despite this, Jeremiah never compromised nor muddied the issues: Judah's sins of external religion were plainly tallied (for example, Jeremiah 7), and the people were urgently reminded in chapter 17 that true religion is a matter of the heart:

"The sin of Judah is written with a pen of iron;
 With the point of a diamond it is engraved
 On the tablet of their heart,
 And on the horns of your altars" (verse 1).

Their external religion was plainly demonstrated in their observance of the Sabbath (verses 19–27), though the right day for the Sabbath was never lost. Verses 20–22 urge, with strong imperatives, obedience to the fourth commandment with a tragic indictment: "Hear the word of the LORD, you kings of Judah, and all Judah, and all the inhabitants of Jerusalem, who enter by these gates. Thus says the LORD: 'Take heed to yourselves, and bear no burden on the Sabbath day, nor bring it in by the gates of Jerusalem; nor carry a burden out of your houses on the Sabbath day, nor do any work, but hallow the Sabbath day, as I commanded your fathers.' "

This instruction was introduced with the verb "hear" (*shema*). (Not unlike the *shema* in Deuteronomy 6:4, 5: "Hear, O Israel: The LORD our God, the LORD is one! You shall love the LORD your God with all your heart, with all your soul, and with all your strength.") In Jeremiah 17:23, Jeremiah twice repeats the same verb: "But they did not obey nor incline their ear, but made their neck stiff, that they might not hear nor receive instruction." Not listening led to grave disobedience.

Following the indictment of verse 23, Jeremiah moves to a double "if-then." Judah is given a fresh chance to decide whether to stay within the covenant by keeping the Sabbath. But if the people violate the Sabbath—and thereby break covenant—there will be massive destruction.

Everything hinges on keeping the Sabbath. It was the test of loyalty to God in Jeremiah's day, and it remains a dramatic sign that God is honored and that the life-giving power of God is trusted. To break the Sabbath means distrusting God and His gifts. The role of the Sabbath is pivotal.

Judah was not condemned for worshiping on a wrong day but for desecrating the right day. God didn't choose lying, adultery, or murder as the test of the covenant, though He could have. He chose remembering the Sabbath day as the covenant seal.

In the book of Lamentations, Jeremiah mournfully recounts the tragedy of the exile and how the divine predictions tragically came true:

How the LORD has covered the daughter of Zion
With a cloud in His anger! (Lamentations 2:1).

The Lord was like an enemy.
He has swallowed up Israel,
He has swallowed up all her palaces;
He has destroyed her strongholds,
And has increased mourning and lamentation
In the daughter of Judah.

He has done violence to His tabernacle,
As if it were a garden;
He has destroyed His place of assembly;
The LORD has caused

The appointed feasts and Sabbaths to be forgotten in Zion (verses 5, 6; emphasis added).

God's justice finally had to punish deliberate human sin and rebellion.

God's wrath is referred to five hundred times in the Old Testament—and numerous times in the book of Revelation. It is only manifested against sin and those who refuse to turn away from it. It never presents God as vindictive, exhibiting petty emotion. God is "slow to anger"—not like we are. And His wrath is displayed only when there is "no remedy," as the chronicler instructed: "But they mocked the messengers of God, despised His words, and scoffed at His prophets, until the wrath of the LORD arose against His people, *till there was no remedy*" (2 Chronicles 36:16; emphasis added).

God is preoccupied with His relationship with His people on the Sabbath. Christians focus more attention on adultery, murder, and lying—and these are serious issues. But God says much more about the Sabbath!

Ezekiel

Through Ezekiel, the prophet during the Babylonian exile, God expressed similar sentiments: "Moreover I also gave them My Sabbaths, to be a sign between them and Me, that they might know that I am the LORD who sanctifies them. Yet the house of Israel rebelled against Me in the wilderness; they did not walk in My statutes; they despised My judgments, 'which, if a man does, he shall live by them'; and they greatly defiled My Sabbaths. Then I said I would pour out My fury on them in the wilderness, to consume them" (Ezekiel 20:12, 13).

Deity reproaches His people many times in this chapter with both grace and curses. He then urges: "I am the LORD your God: Walk in My statutes, keep My judgments, and do them; hallow

My Sabbaths, and they will be a sign between Me and you, that you may know that I am the LORD your God" (verses 19, 20).

Ezekiel has nine references to the Sabbath and its profanation by God's people in chapters 20–23.

Chapter 22 is the section on God's judgment against His people:

- verse 8, they "profaned *My* Sabbaths" (emphasis added)
- verse 26, "they have hidden their eyes from *My* Sabbaths" (emphasis added)
- verse 31, "therefore . . . I have recompensed their deeds" (judgment)

Israel had not distinguished the holy from the unholy—every day is not the same. God destroyed His own temple, and the national existence of His covenant people—and the Sabbath desecration looms large as the reason why. Even though keeping the right day, the people were implying by their actions that it wasn't important to have their hearts linked with the Lord and delighting in Him. From this, we learn that to God, our heart condition and our character are the greatest concern. The Sabbath is not a trivial issue. It is the covenantal sign—a testing matter.

In Ezekiel 25–48, written after the destruction of Jerusalem, the prophet wrote in the hope of the restoration. No different day was to be put in place nor any new theological rationale. Attention was drawn to the historical meaning of the Sabbath—namely, it was a "sign" or pledge of Israel's covenantal relationship with God (Ezekiel 20:10–26). A historical reminder was given—no new innovation was presented.

Ezekiel, divinely commissioned to work with the captives in Babylon, is a prophet of pure grace. Instead of just permitting His people to endure their "earned" punishment, God put Daniel in high government positions to reveal the true God. And to His people, He sent Ezekiel to bring hope.

The Sabbath in Old Testament History and Song

Hosea and Amos

Hosea and Amos describe the same Sabbath problem with the northern ten tribes, Hosea speaking to the generation that suffered Assyrian captivity/exile. Archaeologists have uncovered carved Assyrian panels and tablets that depict the Assyrian treatment of their captives, some even skinned alive—and God will later punish the Assyrians for their cruelty. However, God allowed Israel's degraded religious system to be destroyed, using the Assyrians. The ten tribes' allegiance to God had degenerated into a formalized apostatized system, hollow and empty of heart, and God declared that He could not tolerate it anymore. He had sent many warnings before their final judgment, but all were ignored.

The prophet Hosea also quoted Yahweh warning about Israel's sinfulness and what will result:

"I will also cause all her mirth to cease,
Her feast days,
Her New Moons,
Her Sabbaths—
All her appointed feasts" (Hosea 2:11; emphasis added).

All through the Old Testament, Yahweh always refers to the Sabbath as His, or "Mine." However, Israel's apostasy became so flagrant and evil that He finally called their Sabbaths "hers," for His people refused His rightful Lordship over the Sabbaths. This does not mean the people were worshiping on the wrong day. They always worshiped on the seventh day. But external conformity on the right day was not enough. Their pernicious and pretentious piety was abominable, and Yahweh no longer claimed to be Lord over "their" sabbaths.

Amos, a contemporary of Hosea in the northern tribes (and contemporary with Isaiah and Micah in the south), also described Israel's heartless response to God (Amos 8:1–8). The people were worried that observing the Sabbath would hamper their businesses. After the exile, Nehemiah confronted the same situation.

Prophetic doom messages plainly reveal that God is not looking for nor satisfied with external conformity to His law. He had created His people's worship forms and structure, but observance was to indicate a relationship between them. He is ever unsatisfied with even perfect external conformity if the heart is not there.

Nehemiah and post-captivity Israel

In the time of Nehemiah, the exiles had returned from captivity. The Levites affirmed that the entirety of the Law was conveyed in the observance of the day of rest. They declared their praise to God before all Israel:

> "You came down also on Mount Sinai,
> And spoke with them from heaven,
> And gave them just ordinances and true laws,
> Good statutes and commandments.
> You made known to them Your holy Sabbath,
> And commanded them precepts, statutes and laws,
> By the hand of Moses Your servant" (Nehemiah 9:13, 14).

Nehemiah later scolded the returning captives for again breaking the Sabbath. He reminded them that it was the major sin that lay behind their Babylonian exile: "Then I contended with the nobles of Judah, and said to them, 'What evil thing is this that you do, by which you profane the Sabbath day? Did not your fathers do thus, and did not our God bring all this disaster on us and on this city? Yet you bring added wrath on Israel by profaning the Sabbath' " (Nehemiah 13:17, 18).

The Old Testament closes with the prophet Malachi presenting the same divine sentiments:

"Remember the Law of Moses, My servant,
Which I commanded him in Horeb for all Israel,
With the statutes and judgments.
Behold, I will send you Elijah the prophet
Before the coming of the great and dreadful day of the Lord.
And he will turn
The hearts of the fathers to the children,
And the hearts of the children to their fathers,
Lest I come and strike the earth with a curse" (Malachi
    4:4–6).

This time the entire law is referred to—and its remembrance divinely urged! And once again, true obedience is a matter of the heart! All the prophets called for "heart reform" when discussing Sabbath keeping.

The divine way of life extolled by the prophets was not a special role for a select few but instead is at the heart of a fully responsible human life. The prophets were not only about making grim predictions. They also called for a powerful way of life that will restore the image of God in His people as they faithfully follow Him. And such a blessed person will find his or her life spent responding to others' needs. Just as Yahweh is always giving, so those who are redeemed and renewed will respond to others' needs. The divine impulse nurtures and inspires responsibility and loving care. It presupposes the value of every person, cherishing each one as God's child just as the Creator Himself does. The prophets described this quality of life flowing from those who delight in the Lord and His Sabbath.

The Sabbath day and lessons of its nature and beauty are woven throughout the Old Testament. Nothing changed in the New Testament—to where we will journey after a brief survey of the intertestamental period and the milieu of the first-century world when Jesus lived on earth. This will help inform our understanding of why Jesus said what He said and did what He did concerning the Sabbath. We will also observe how His disciples continued to treasure the Sabbath.

1. J. Clinton McCann Jr., *A Theological Introduction to the Book of Psalms: The Psalms as Torah* (Nashville, TN: Abingdon, 1993), 29.

2. Ellen G. White, *Early Writings* (Washington, DC: Review and Herald®, 1945), 190, 191.

3. John Calvin, *Institutes of the Christian Religion* (Philadelphia, PA: Westminster, 1950), 396.

4. Nahum M. Sarna, "The Psalm for the Sabbath Day (Ps 92)," *Journal of Biblical Literature* 81, no. 2 (June 1962): 158–168.

5. Abraham Joshua Heschel, *The Sabbath* (New York: Farrar, Straus and Giroux, 2005), 22.

6. Ellen G. White, *The Desire of Ages* (Mountain View, CA: Pacific Press®, 1940), 281, 282.

7. Ellen G. White, *Patriarchs and Prophets* (Mountain View, CA: Pacific Press®, 1958), 72; emphasis in original.

Chapter Three

The Intertestamental Period:
What Happened?

At the close of the book of Malachi, the last book of the Old Testament, there follow what are called four hundred years of "prophetic silence," broken only with the powerful voice of John the Baptist as the New Testament record opens.

Sometimes referred to as late Judaism, this four-hundred-year period preceded the time of Jesus' earthly ministry. Several different Jewish groups had come into existence. Only two of these survived the destruction of the temple in AD 70: Christianity and Pharisaism.

Gathering and preserving Jewish tradition after the temple's destruction proved foundational for preserving Judaism. After its destruction, there was no place for the temple system to be carried out. This called for major adjustments for everyone, including surviving Pharisees. The intertestamental period of Pharisaism came to be referred to (post AD 70) as Rabbinic Judaism—with modern forms of Judaism emerging from it. Unfortunately, it developed into a double apostasy of both the law and the gospel— and the true glories of both were lost. Laws were written about laws again and again. In the process, the gift of the gospel was reduced to high human achievement.

Sometime after AD 135, Rabbi Meir made a compilation of the oral laws known to him. These oral laws were already operant in Judaism in the time of Jesus—and appraising them illuminates the religious climate Jesus was working within and informing what He did. To this collection, more was added. And at the beginning of the third century, Rabbi Judah the Prince prepared the basic codification of Rabbinic law known as the Mishnah, which still remains the foundational guide for orthodox Jewish life. It is as vital to understanding Judaism as the New Testament is to understanding first-century Christianity.

The Mishnah consists of sixty-three books, or "tractates," each dealing with a different subject. The tractates dealing primarily with the Sabbath laws are entitled *Shabbat* and *Erubin*. *Shabbat* is the first tractate of the Mishnah, consisting of twenty-four chapters. It deals with laws relating to Shabbat (the weekly day of rest) and thirty-nine *melakhot*, or activities, prohibited on Shabbat. *Shabbat* is the longest tractate in the Mishnah, and the subject is also dealt with in other tractates.

"No other institution is more important to Judaism than the Sabbath, and only circumcision comes near to equaling it. The rabbis regarded the Sabbath as equaling in importance [as] all other precepts of the Torah combined."[1] For example: "It was said, 'He who observes the Sabbath is kept far from sin.' "[2] One rabbi suggested that the Lord said, " 'O My people, behold, you have annulled all Ten Commandments. Nevertheless, if you had kept one Commandment . . . I would have forgiven you. And which Commandment is this? It is the Commandment concerning the Sabbath Day.' "[3]

Not only was the Sabbath an essential feature of Jewish identity, but it was also regarded as a way of witnessing about the Creator. It was said: "The Sabbath adds holiness to Israel. Why is the shop of Ben-David closed? Because he keeps the Sabbath. Why does Ben-David abstain from work? Because he keeps the Sabbath. He thus bears witness to Him by whose word the world came into being that He created His world in six days and rested on the seventh. And thus it says: 'Therefore ye are My witnesses, saith the LORD, and I am God' (Isaiah 43:12)."

"Cardinal gifts of privileges, blessings, and deliverances were promised to Israel as a reward for success in Sabbathkeeping. Above all, the final redemption was said to hinge upon correct observance of the Sabbath. Rabbi Johanan said in the name of Simeon ben Yohai: 'If Israel were to keep two Sabbaths according to the laws thereof, they would be redeemed immediately.' Rabbi Levi said: 'If Israel kept the Sabbath properly even for one day, the son of David would come. Why? Because it is equivalent to all the commandments.' "[4]

Isaiah 30:15 was cited to show that true repentance ("returning") and Sabbath keeping ("rest") were the conditions of salvation, the way to hasten the coming of the Messiah. In the Jewish Haggadah (text for celebrating the Passover), Simeon ben Lakish discusses the Sabbath: "It is the way of the world that even a king who considers himself enlightened might say to his servants: 'Work one day for yourselves and six days for me.' Not so the Holy One, blessed be He. This is what the Holy One, blessed be He, says to Israel: 'My children, keep six days for yourselves, and keep only one day for Me.' "

It became the custom of many Jews to follow the example attributed to the first-century Rabbi Hanina, who donned his best robe and stood at sunset at the beginning of the Sabbath, exclaiming, "Come and let us go forth to welcome the queen Sabbath." Also, Rabbi Jannai, who attired himself similarly, met the Sabbath with the words, "Come, O bride, come, O bride!"*

"The Sabbath is seen as an island of eternity within time, a foretaste of the world to come. Tamid 7.4 declares that Psalm 92

---

* The Hebrew word for "bride" (*kallah*) sounds the same as the word used to describe God completing His work of creation in Genesis 2:1. The royal aspect comes from Isaiah 58, where the Sabbath is called a "[royal] delight." The word used is one of the dozen Hebrew words rightly translated "delight," but this one is used only with royalty in their palaces. Thus the more complete meaning in Isaiah suggests that the Sabbath is a "royal delight"!

["A Song for the Sabbath"], the psalm sung by the Levites in the Temple on Sabbath is 'a song for the time that is to come, for the day that shall be all Sabbath and rest in the life everlasting.' "[5]

More verbs are connected with the creation of the Sabbath than any other day of the week ("finishing," "resting," "blessing," "hallowing"). So when the rabbis sought to explain God's activity on the Sabbath in light of the stipulation in the fourth commandment of "not doing any work," the rabbis decided that since "it is written, 'do not I fill heaven and earth?' (Jeremiah 23:24)," God couldn't be accused of carrying anything. Another explanation was the work that was permitted to be done on the Sabbath within the sanctuary—the whole universe seen as God's temple. Against this background, Jesus' statement during a Sabbath controversy with the religious leaders is notable: "My Father is working still, and I am working" (John 5:17, RSV).

Reading rabbinic literature gives a sense of the ancient rabbinical context. The rabbis wrote in terms of things permitted and things forbidden—a way to labor through the world's confusion from birth to death and avoid bumping into any walls. Their writings are a type of legal literature, detailing what may or may not be done, sounding nothing like Greek philosophy, which had reached a high point by the time of Christ.

The Sabbath was presented as a gift. Every Friday night the Sabbath was inaugurated with the phrase "*Shabbat kodsho . . . hinchilanu*": "You have given us Your holy Shabbat as an inheritance." Similarly, "You did not give it to the nations of the world, nor give it as an inheritance to idolators; rather to Your people Israel You gave it, in love" (author's translation).[6]

Later in the same prayer, the verb *nchi* appears, not in the perfect, but an imperative—a petition that God would continue to give them the Sabbath as their heritage. The indicative verb form implied that the Sabbath was a gift of God's grace, with the imperative implying that the continuation of the Sabbath as Israel's gift was contingent—something which God gives but could be removed the moment a person is unworthy of the gift.

The only ritual that superseded the Sabbath was circumcision, which had to take place on the eighth day after birth. Rabbi Jose the Galilean said: "Great is circumcision, for it sets aside the Sabbath, which is very important and the profanation of which is punishable by extinction."[7]

To deal with possible complex situations, the rabbis defined distinct guidelines. "If the eighth day fell on the Sabbath, even the necessary preparations for the operation [of circumcision] were lawful."[8] All the same, "Rabbi Akiba laid down the rule: 'Any act of work that can be done on the eve of the Sabbath does not override the Sabbath, but what cannot be done on the eve of the Sabbath [for ceremonial purposes] overrides the Sabbath.' "[9]

However, this was allowed only if the birth had clearly taken place during the previous Sabbath, in which case the eighth day would also be a Sabbath. If the timing was doubtful, such as if the boy were born at twilight Friday, the circumcision was put off until Sunday.

The rabbis clearly viewed the Decalogue Sabbath as one of Deity's great gifts. Many thought of it as a taste of eternity in this world.[10] God did give the Sabbath as an important gift, yet its sanctity needed to be preserved. Problems developed in the instructions devised for preserving its holiness.

The rabbis believed that the Sabbath (and the law in general) was so important that a fence was needed to surround and protect it. To ensure that no one could violate the Sabbath in any way, the rabbis constructed a fence of rules around it, reasoning that the fence would protect the Sabbath from any violations. Their original motive was honorable—to guard the law. The result, however, was an ever-increasing number of fences built to protect the fences. This collection of "fences" in their oral tradition was eventually written down in the Mishnah, seeking to define correct Sabbath observance for every conceivable situation.

The process became endless. Once a rule was made for one situation, exceptions and special cases arose from it that also needed to be dealt with. After that, more exceptions to the exceptional cases came up—with no end to the intricate distinctions. Rabbis sought to ensure that everyone would act so circumspectly that no one would even come close to breaking the Sabbath. But eventually, so many fences were built to protect the previous fences that the Sabbath itself was lost sight of, and protecting the fences became the main focus.

For example, to ensure that no work be done on the Sabbath, the rabbis attempted to define work by determining thirty-nine major classes of it. They derived this list from all the types of work that would have been necessary to construct the sanctuary, declaring

> the main classes of work are forty save one: sowing, ploughing, reaping, binding sheaves, threshing, winnowing, cleansing crops, grinding, sifting, kneading, baking, shearing wool, washing or beating or dyeing it, spinning, weaving, making two loops, weaving two threads, separating two threads, tying [a knot], loosening [a knot], sewing two stitches, . . . hunting a gazelle, slaughtering or flaying or salting it or curing its skin, scraping it or cutting it up, writing two letters, erasing in order to write two letters, building, pulling down, putting out a fire, lighting a fire, striking with a hammer and taking out aught from one domain into another. These are the main classes of work: forty save one.[11]

But even these definitions did not suffice. Special cases arose, which resulted in more rules with debates among the rabbis themselves as to just where to draw the line.

For instance, at the beginning of the first century (the time of

Jesus), two famous rabbis, Hillel and Shammai, argued whether a Jew could

- help a Gentile load his donkey on a weekday if the Gentile intended to travel so far that he would not arrive before Sabbath[12] or
- eat eggs that a hen had laid on Sabbath.[13]

Another case of attempting to define Sabbath observance for every situation involved the rule on how one should keep the Sabbath if their house caught on fire. This would present various problems for the owner, including putting out a fire and carrying things, both of which were prohibited on Sabbath. However, the rabbis formulated exceptions for the specific case of the burning house:

- One could carry food out of the house—enough for three meals for each member of the household.
- One could not *carry* clothes but could *put on* as many clothes as possible and *wear* them out of the burning house.
- Putting out the fire was not allowed, but if a Gentile volunteered to put out the fire, a good Jew could allow him to do so; one could not, however, ask a Gentile to put it out.[14]

Another attempt to spell out precise distinctions for proper Sabbath keeping involved camels: a person could lead one camel with a rope on Sabbath but not tie several camels' ropes together. However, one could lead several camels if each one was led by a separate rope. But the person must hold each rope separately, for if the ropes in one hand twisted into a knot, the camels would be considered tied together and in violation of the law.[15]

We are so far removed from the period of Late Judaism that these distinctions seem petty to us. But we must remember that it was a part of a serious attempt to preserve the sacredness of the Sabbath—and to protect anyone from violating it. In fact, the rabbis were trying to be reasonable. That's why they spelled out all the exceptions. Jesus Himself commended the Pharisees for allowing the lifting out of an animal from a pit on the Sabbath, though this might entail vigorous work (Luke 14:1–6). Members of the Dead Sea Scrolls community were stricter: their law explicitly said: "No man shall assist a beast to give birth on the Sabbath day. And if it should fall into a cistern or pit, he shall not lift it out on the Sabbath."[16]

Attempting to be reasonable on the one hand and yet becoming extremely strict on the other can be seen in the rabbis' attitudes toward tending the sick on the Sabbath. As a general rule, they forbade healing practices and administering medicine as being work.[17] This again led to intricate distinctions. The rabbis both permitted and forbade the same act or the use of certain substances on the Sabbath in different situations. It all depended on whether or not the individual used it medicinally or how sick the person was:

- If his teeth pain him, he may not suck vinegar through them, but he may take vinegar after his usual fashion, and if he is healed, he is healed.
- If his loins pain him, he may not rub thereon wine or vinegar, yet he may anoint them with oil but not with rose-oil. King's children may anoint their wounds with rose-oil since it is their custom to do so on ordinary days.[18]
- If a man's hand or foot is dislocated, he may not pour cold water over it, but he may wash it after his usual fashion, and if he is healed, he is healed.[19]
- "If a man has a pain in his throat they may not drop medicine into his mouth on the Sabbath, since there is doubt whether life is in danger, and whenever there is doubt whether life is in danger this overrides the Sabbath."[20]

The Intertestamental Period: What Happened?

The rabbis believed they were being reasonable. While generally outlawing healing practices, they made an exception when there was an actual danger of loss of life. Human life was considered of equal value to the Sabbath.

Rabbinic rules also granted exceptions for assisting in childbirth, as was done for performing circumcision on the Sabbath. In fact, one could even put out a candle on Sabbath (otherwise forbidden) if it would help a very sick person get some needed sleep. The rabbis manifested concern for the sick if life was in danger.

They also reasoned that Moses received both the moral and general laws, which became Israel's "tradition," at the same time, and from the same Author as the moral law. The moral law was written by God's own finger into stone with the others communicated orally to Moses. The rabbis decided there needed to be a third authority to harmonize these two sets of laws. And the Pharisees took on the task of doing this.

This is what had happened to the Sabbath in Jesus' day. The well-meaning attempts to protect the Sabbath by defining its observance in every situation had hidden its true glory. The fences no longer protected the people from violating the Sabbath. Instead, it shut them out of it. This helps explain why Christ challenged pharisaical legalism. He was trying to provoke the issue of true Sabbath keeping—not to correct which day was the Sabbath. Late Judaism expresses the prominent religious sentiments Jesus was working with and what He was confronting. He was trying to open up the issue of what true Sabbath keeping is in an effort to restore the true glory of the day.

Recall Jesus' strong statement when responding to the scribes and Pharisees who had complained to Him, "Why do Your disciples transgress the tradition of the elders?" (Matthew 15:2). Notice, they didn't complain that the disciples were transgressing the Old Testament—only the "tradition of the elders." Jesus' response clarifies the problem:

"Thus you have made the commandment of God of no effect by your tradition. Hypocrites! Well did Isaiah prophesy about you saying:

'These people draw near to Me with their mouth,
And honor Me with their lips,
But their heart is far from Me.
And in vain they worship Me,
Teaching as doctrines the commandments of men' " (verses 6–9).

Jesus was not condemning upholding doctrine—He was only insisting that all human interpretation of doctrine needs to be continually informed and corrected by Scripture.

For the religious leaders of Late Judaism, human laws took precedence over God's laws. Transgression of Jewish laws was more serious than the transgression of God's law. In fact, the supposedly "protective fences" around God's law were so high and so thick they were impenetrable, completely obscuring the law of God they were supposed to be guarding.

Fulfilling the numerous written commandments regarding the Sabbath was also regarded as gaining merit with God. The original divine prohibitions against work were now interpreted to include other activities:

- A person can't roast eggs in the sand because this involves the process of moving the soil to bury the eggs, and this would be "plowing."
- Nor can a lamp be tilted to get better light even to read Scripture.
- A person cannot look in a mirror because it might make him or her want to remove a white hair.
- Taking a bath was not permitted because a towel might need to be wrung out.

The Intertestamental Period: What Happened?

The many laws and many cases of what one could or could not do took away any necessity for study or decision-making. Keeping the Sabbath had grown into carrying a complex moral yoke—and in the process stymied each person's moral development. This resulted in making God the Lawgiver a tyrant, and obedience became a matter of external conformity needing no heart relationship. This all led to a religion of salvation by works.

Instead of the law being a mirror showing us how much we need a Savior and the cleansing He longs to give, it became a heavy yoke that Jesus desired to replace with His grace. Instead of the gospel, there emerged a theological legalism replacing a vital, living relationship with the Savior. No salvation messages were found in the sanctuary services which were so proudly and rigidly observed.

Even so, we should appreciate the high regard of the rabbis for the law, which motivated their legalistic observance of it—especially in this time when the law is widely thought to be done away with. Additionally, we should not criticize all the Pharisees. Two Pharisees mentioned in the gospels were sincere seekers of truth:

- Nicodemus came to see Jesus and listen to Him personally (John 3). Later, he called for fairness in the treatment of Jesus (John 7, especially verses 50, 51), and even later, he was one of the few brave enough to be seen at Jesus' tomb (John 19:38–40).
- "Now behold, there was a man named *Joseph, a council member, a good and just man.* He had not consented to their decision and deed. He was from Arimathea, a city of the Jews, who himself was also waiting for the kingdom of God" (Luke 23:50, 51; emphasis added). The Gospel of Mark provides more details: "Now when evening had come, because it was the Preparation Day, that is, the day before the Sabbath, *Joseph of Arimathea, a prominent council*

member, who was himself waiting for the kingdom of God, coming and taking courage, went in to Pilate and asked for the body of Jesus" (Mark 15:42, 43; emphasis added).

Moreover, the first-century Pharisees were more moderate than other contemporary Jewish factions—those who considered that they were attempting, as the faithful, holy remnant, to continue the reformation of Ezra. Even more radical were the Essenes, who had very strict rules covering everything from bathing to baptizing. A person could not join this last group if he or she were not physically perfect.

The Pharisees were not so extreme. But, according to the Gospels, Jesus was most often confronted by them as He sought to remove their Sabbath-smothering traditions. He regarded the Sabbath very highly and wanted to eliminate their impenetrable barrier between the true biblical Sabbath and Jewish tradition.

Could it be that some modern Seventh-day Adventists go to the opposite extreme, not respecting the Sabbath as holy time that needs to be carefully guarded, doing nothing to preserve its glory or protect its blessing?

The situation in Late Judaism only got worse. Some writings had extreme interpretations of the early Hassidim, at the time of Antiochus Epiphanes:

- The Book of Jubilees forbade making war on Sabbath; sexual expressions of love between husband and wife, and travel, on pain of capital punishment.
- The Document of Daniel forbade saving an animal's life— or even a human being if the use of a rope or ladder was needed.
- The Fragment of Zadokites forbade lending to a visitor on Sabbath.

The Intertestamental Period: What Happened?

Extrabiblical records

Extrabiblical historical records also mention the Sabbath. The first-century Greek-speaking Jewish writer in Alexandria, Philo (a contemporary of Jesus living in Egypt), described the Sabbath: "On this day we are commanded to abstain from all work, not because the law inculcates slackness. . . . Its object is rather to give man relaxation from continuous and unending toil and by refreshing their bodies with a regularly calculated system of remissions to send them out renewed to their old activities. For a breathing spell enables not merely ordinary people but athletes also to collect their strength with a stronger force behind them to undertake promptly and patiently each of the tasks set before them."[21]

Philo's discussion presents the Sabbath more like a Greek philosophical subject: the Sabbath is for the sake of gaining strength of activity, not spiritual renewal. In Scripture, the Sabbath is more than just becoming more fit for next week's labor, though it can have that effect. Rather, it is a day of renewal and restoration with the Creator—truly a gift of grace. God is not a despot, and humans are not His slaves.

Philo also described prayer houses or meeting houses where the Jews met weekly to read and study their laws.[22] The situation he presented was similar to the philosophical schools of the Greeks: "Each seventh day there stand wide open in every city thousands of schools of good sense, . . . in which the scholars sit . . . with full attention."[23] He continues that those present sat "together in a respectful and orderly manner" and heard "the laws read so that none should be ignorant of them."[24]

He also wrote about the Sabbath religious activities of the Therapeutae, which sound more worshipful: those in attendance "do not confine themselves to contemplation but also compose hymns and psalms" and "every seventh day they meet together as for a general assembly and sit . . . in the proper attitude."[25]

Philo also mentioned the Sabbath of the Essenes, who went on the Sabbath to sacred spots that, he wrote, "they called synagogues. There they listened to books read aloud and discourses."[26] He also writes of the Jews in Egypt assembling in *synagogia* (gatherings), which were schools of temperance and justice. The word *synagogue*, which Philo used, is also found in the Gospels and the book of Acts (65 times). He linked the Sabbath to the Creation in *De cherubim*:

> And on this account too Moses calls the Sabbath, which name being interpreted means "rest," "the sabbath of God." [Leviticus 23:2] Touching upon the necessary principles of natural philosophy, not of the philosophy of men, in many parts of his law, for that among existing things which rests, if one must tell the truth, is one thing only, God. And by "rest" I do not mean "inaction" (since that which is by its nature energetic, that which is the cause of all things, can never desist from doing what is most excellent), but I mean an energy completely free from labor, without any feeling of sufferings, and with the most perfect ease.[27]

Affirming the great benefit of the Sabbath, he wrote: "Again, those who properly keep the sacred Sabbath are benefitted in two most important particulars, both body and soul; as to their body, by a rest from their continual and incessant labors; and as to their soul, by forming most excellent conceptions respecting God as the Creator of the universe and the careful protector of all the things and beings which and whom he has made. And he made the whole universe in one week. It is plain, therefore, from these things that the man who honors the seventh day will himself find honor."[28]

The Jewish historian Josephus wrote toward the end of the first-century AD about the origin of the Sabbath: "Accordingly Moses says, That in just six days the world, and all that is therein, was made. And that the seventh day was a rest, and a release from the labor of such operations; whence it is that we celebrate a rest from our labors on that day, and call it the Sabbath, which word denotes rest in the Hebrew tongue."[29]

Later he goes to describe how the Jews in the time of the Maccabees came to accept defensive fighting on the Sabbath, beginning with a description of Jews who refused to fight on the Sabbath:

And they avoided to defend themselves on that day, because they were not willing to break in upon the honor they owed the Sabbath, even in such distresses; for our law requires that we rest upon that day. There were about a thousand, with their wives and children, who were smothered and died in these caves; but many of those who escaped joined themselves to Mattathias, and appointed him to be their ruler, who taught them to fight, even on the sabbath day; and told them that unless they would do so, they would become their own enemies, by observing the law [so rigorously], while their adversaries would still assault them on this day, and they would not then defend themselves, and that nothing could then hinder but they must all perish without fighting. This speech persuaded them. And this rule continues among us to this day, that if there be a necessity, we may fight on sabbath days.[30]

Josephus also mentioned an incident in the synagogue at Caesarea: the Jews there were taunted by the local citizens. Once these citizens discovered that the Jews would be offended, they deliberately slaughtered birds at the entrance to the synagogue on the Sabbath.[31] And he wrote about a synagogue in Antioch that had enough prestige to receive, from Antiochus, the returned plundered votive brass vessels from the Jerusalem temple.[32] In another narrative, he referred to the prayer house (*proseucha*) at Tiberias as a large meeting place and gave a description of prayer houses similar to the accounts of Philo.[33]

Rediscovering the Glory the Sabbath

Archaeological evidence for the Sabbath includes the Theodotus inscription—often referred to as proof for the existence of a synagogue in Jerusalem in the first century AD. The inscription commemorates a man who ruled the synagogue along with his grandfather, who had built it and acted as its ruler before him. It describes a building in which the reading of the law and the teaching of the commandments took place and also mentions that the synagogue had a hospitality suite with water fittings for the use of travelers.

When the Romans commented on the Jews' strict adherence to the law of abstaining from labor on the Sabbath, it was with a contempt similar to Pharaoh's in ancient Egypt.

"The God of the Hebrews has met with us. Please, let us go three days' journey into the desert and sacrifice to the LORD our God, lest He fall upon us with pestilence or with the sword."

Then the king of Egypt said to them, "Moses and Aaron, why do you take the people from their work? Get back to your labor." And Pharaoh said, "Look, the people of the land are many now, and you make them rest from their labor!"

So the same day Pharaoh commanded the taskmasters of the people and their officers, saying, "You shall no longer give the people straw to make brick as before. Let them go and gather straw for themselves. And you shall lay on them the quota of bricks which they made before. You shall not reduce it. For they are idle; therefore they cry out, saying, 'Let us go and sacrifice to our God.' Let more work be laid on the men, that they may labor in it, and let them not regard false words" (Exodus 5:3–9).

The Sabbath was called a "sign of Jewish indolence" by Juvenal, Seneca, and others. Listen to a few Greco-Roman writers speaking about the seventh-day Sabbath:

- *Agatharchides of Cnidus, second century BC.* "The people known as Jews . . . have a custom of abstaining from work every seventh day; on those occasions they neither bear arms nor take any agricultural operations in hand, nor engage in any other form of public service, but pray with outstretched hands in the temples until the evening." He goes on to strongly rebuke the Jewish practice of Sabbath keeping as the reason of the fall of Palestine to Ptolemy.[34]
- *Apion, early first century AD.* Apion attributes the origin of the name "Sabbath" to the Exodus: "After a six days' march, . . . they developed tumours in the groin, and that was why, after safely reaching the country now called Judaea, they rested on the seventh day, and called that day *sabbaton*, preserving the Egyptian terminology; for disease of the groin in Egypt is called *sabbo*."[35]
- *Petronius, first century AD.* Petronius mentions a somewhat common misconception then of the Sabbath as a day of fasting (though the only day on which Jews fast is the Day of Atonement, Yom Kippur): "The Jew may worship his pig-god and clamor in the ears of high heaven, but unless he also cuts back his foreskin with the knife, he shall go forth from the people and emigrate to Greek cities, and shall not tremble at the fasts of Sabbath imposed by the law."[36]
- *Juvenal, AD 60–130.* Juvenal sees the Sabbath as a wasted day of idleness. Referring to Gentiles who take on Sabbath observance, he states: "Some who have had a father who reveres the Sabbath, worship nothing but the clouds. . . . Having been wont to flout the laws of Rome, they learn and practise and revere the Jewish law. . . . For all which the father was to blame, who gave up every seventh day to idleness, keeping it apart from all the concerns of life."[37]

- *Plutarch, first to second century AD.* Plutarch speaks of the Sabbath in regard to military defense: "But the Jews, because it was the Sabbath day, sat in their places immovable, while the enemy were planting ladders against the walls and capturing the defenses, and they did not get up, but remained there, fast bound in the toils of superstition as in one great net."[38] He further comments while quoting Moeragenes: "I believe that even the feast of the Sabbath is not completely unrelated to Dionysus. Many even now call the Bacchants *Sabi* and utter that cry when celebrating the god. . . . The Jews themselves testify to a connection with Dionysus when they keep the Sabbath by inviting each other to drink and to enjoy wine."[39]

Notice three common misconceptions in these excerpts:

- false understanding of the origin and practice of the Sabbath
- prejudice against the Jews and their customs
- assumption that the reader is unacquainted with the Jewish Sabbath and needs to be informed (even though the arguments are incorrect)

Many Greco-Roman writers held predominantly negative attitudes toward Jewish beliefs and practices, which suggests incomplete knowledge of them. For example, Juvenal counted "all the concerns of life" as more important than devoting "every seventh day to idleness."

We have now taken time to survey various extrabiblical sources to better understand the first-century world Jesus entered—to where we next proceed.

The Intertestamental Period: What Happened?

1. Hullin 5a; J. Berakoth 1:5; J. Nedarim 3:14; Ex. R. 25: 12; Deut. R. 4:4, cited in Robert Johnston, "The Rabbinic Sabbath," in *The Sabbath in Scripture and History*, ed. Kenneth A. Strand (Hagerstown, MD: Review and Herald®, 1982), 71.

2. Mek. Vayassa' 6, quoted in Robert Johnston, "The Rabbinic Sabbath," 71.

3. Pesikta Rabbati 27:4, quoted in Hullin 5a; J. Berakoth 1:5; J. Nedarim 3:14; Ex. R. 25:12; Deut. R. 4:4, cited in Johnston, "The Rabbinic Sabbath," 71.

4. Mek. Shabbata 1; Shab. 118b; Ex. R. 25:12; J. Taanith 1:1, quoted in Johnston, "The Rabbinic Sabbath," 72.

5. Rosh ba-Shanah 1:4, 5, 9, quoted in Johnston, "The Rabbinic Sabbath," 73.

6. "Kiddush for Evening of Shabbat," in *Mishkan T'Filah: A Reform Siddur*, ed. Elyse D. Frishman, Shabbat, Nontransliterated Edition (New York: Central Conference of American Rabbis, 2007), 5.

7. Mek. Amalek 3, quoted in Johnston, "The Rabbinic Sabbath," 75.

8. Johnston, "The Rabbinic Sabbath," 75.

9. Shab. 19:5, quoted in Johnston, "The Rabbinic Sabbath," 75.

10. Tamid 7:4, in Herbert Danby, trans., *The Mishnah* (New York: Oxford University Press, 1933), 589.

11. Shabbath 7:2, in Danby, *The Mishnah*, 106.

12. Shabbath 1:7, in Danby, *The Mishnah*, 101.

13. Eduyoth 4:1, in Danby, *The Mishnah*, 428.

14. Shabbath 16:1–6, in Danby, *The Mishnah*, 114.

15. Shabbath 5:1–3, in Danby, *The Mishnah*, 104.

16. G. Vermes, trans., *The Dead Sea Scrolls in English*, 2nd ed. (Baltimore: Penguin Books, 1975), 113.

17. *Shabbath* 10:1; Danby, 109.

18. *Shabbath* 14:4; Danby, 113.

19. *Shabbath* 22:6; Danby, 119.

20. Yoma 8:6, in Danby, *The Mishnah*, 172.

21. Philo, *On the Special Laws* 2.15:59, in F. H. Colson, trans., *Philo*, vol. 7, Loeb Classics Library (Cambridge, MA: Harvard University Press, 1998).

22. Philo, *On the Embassy to Gaius* 132–137, 156–167, *Against Flaccus* 41–50.

23. Philo, *On the Special Laws* 2.15.62, in Colson, *Philo*, vol. 7, 347.

24. Philo, *Hypothetica* 7.12, in F. H. Colson, trans., *Philo*, vol. 4, Loeb Classical Library (Cambridge, MA: Harvard University Press, 1985), 433.

25. Philo, *On the Contemplative Life* 3.29, 30, in F. H. Colson, trans., *Philo*, vol. 9, Loeb Classical Library (Cambridge, MA: Harvard University Press, 1985), 129, 131.

26. Philo, *That Every Good Person Is Free*, 12:81–83.

27. Philo, *On the cherubim* 1.26:87 (Yonge, Early Christian Writings), http://www.earlychristianwritings.com/yonge/book5.html.

28. Philo, *Spec. Laws* 2.48:260 (Yonge, Early Christian Writings), http://www.early christianwritings.com/yonge/book28.html.

29. Josephus, *Jewish Antiquities* 1.33 (Whiston), http://www.perseus.tufts.edu/hopper /text?doc=Perseus:text:1999.01.0146:book=1:section=27&highlight=sabbath.

30. Josephus, *Ant.* 12.274–277.

31. Josephus, *Jewish War* 2.284–293 (Whiston), http://www.perseus.tufts.edu/hopper

/text?doc=Perseus%3Atext%3A1999.01.0148%3Abook%3D2%3Asection%3D289.

32. Josephus, *Ant.* 16.40–46.

33. Josephus, *Against Apion*, 173–177, 277–287; *The Life* 272–282 (Whiston) http://www.perseus.tufts.edu/hopper/text?doc=Perseus%3Atext%3A1999.01.0150%3 Asection%3D276.

34. Encyclopedia.com, s.v. "Agatharchides of Cnidus," updated May 13, 2020, https://www.encyclopedia.com/religion/encyclopedias-almanacs-transcripts-and-maps /agatharchides-cnidusdeg.

35. Flavius Josephus, *Against Apion* 2.21, in H. St. J. Thackeray, trans., *Josephus*, vol. 1, Loeb Classical Library (New York: G. P. Putnam's Sons, 1926), 301.

36. Petronius *Fragments*, no. 37. See also Marital, writing in the second half of the first century AD, *Epigrammata*, II, 2; and Tacitus, *Historiae*, V.4.3.

37. Juvenal, *Satire* 14.96–106, in G. G. Ramsay, trans., *Juvenal and Persius*, Loeb Classical Library (New York: G. P. Putnam's Sons, 1918), 271, 273.

38. Plutarch, *De Superstitione*, 8:169C.

39. Plutarch, *Quaestionum convivialum libri IV*, 6:2:671E–672A.

Chapter Four

The Lord of the Sabbath:
His Day and His Disciples

Though celebrating the Christmas season is presently a high point of the calendar year, only two of the four New Testament Gospels mention it—Matthew and Luke. Mark and John open their Gospels with Jesus as an adult. However, all four Gospels highlight the ministry of John the Baptist.

After four hundred years of prophetic silence, John the Baptist burst on the scene, crying out for repentance—even of religious leaders. He also proclaimed the coming of the Messiah, the "Lamb of God who takes away the sin of the world" (John 1:29). His influence was so powerful that some wondered whether John was the promised prophet that Moses had predicted: "The people were in expectation, and all reasoned in their hearts about John, whether he was the Christ or not" (Luke 3:15; cf. Deuteronomy 18:15).

But John ever insisted that he was preparing the way for the Messiah as Isaiah had foretold:

The voice of one crying in the wilderness:
"Prepare the way of the LORD;
Make straight in the desert
A highway for our God" (Isaiah 40:3; see Matthew 3:3).

Even with this impressive introduction, Jesus, during His short three and a half years of public ministry, was usually surrounded by hostile religious leaders who didn't want Him to be the Messiah. And much of their hostility toward Him related to how He kept the Sabbath. Not because Jesus or the Jews were worshiping on the wrong day—that never was an issue.

All four Gospels provide narratives of Jesus and His Sabbath—often including accounts of the fierce anger it drew from the religious leaders. Understanding why Jesus was attacked for His Sabbath keeping is crucial when reading the Gospels. He simply would not bow to any human tradition. In the Old Testament, He had called the Sabbath "My holy day" (Isaiah 58:13)—and He never relinquished His ownership throughout His life on earth, even though it cost Him His life. He even dared to accuse the religious leaders of breaking the commandments:

"Well did Isaiah prophesy of you hypocrites, as it is written:

'This people honors Me with their lips,
But their heart is far from Me.
And in vain they worship Me,
Teaching as doctrines the commandments of men.'

For laying aside the commandment of God, you hold the tradition of men . . ."
He said to them, "All too well you reject the commandment of God, that you may keep your tradition" (Mark 7:6–9).

Luke is the only "Gentile" who contributed to the New Testament, and he referred to Jesus and the Sabbath more than the three Jewish Gospel writers. It must have impressed him: he used the word *Sabbath* twenty-one times in his Gospel and eight times in the book of Acts.

In Luke's Gospel, we find Jesus habitually kept the Sabbath—"as

The Lord of the Sabbath: His Day and His Disciples

His custom was" (e.g., Luke 4:16). Luke also recorded how Jesus inaugurated His public ministry on a Sabbath morning in the synagogue (Luke 4:14–30). He then immediately connected this announcement to two of Jesus' Sabbath miracles. In this way, Luke underscored the verity of Jesus' Messianic proclamations fulfilling Old Testament prophecies.

When Jesus made His dramatic announcement in Nazareth that Sabbath morning, He quoted from Isaiah 58 and 61, which contained the ancient treasured Messianic promises outlining the pattern of the Messiah's ministry that the Jews had been pinning their hopes on for centuries.

Isaiah 58 promised the restoration of the Sabbath, with Isaiah 61 forging a connection of the Sabbath with salvation. And all during His public ministry, Jesus earnestly sought to restore the gospel's luster by connecting it with the Sabbath's original blessing. Jesus' short three-year public ministry schedule was always bustling. It included teaching His disciples, preaching to large crowds, private "tutoring" of Nicodemus (John 3) and the woman at Samaria's well (John 4), and performing many miracles. Sometimes all the sick and infirm of a whole village or town would be healed as Jesus passed through (see Matthew 4:24; Matthew 12:15; Luke 5:15; Luke 6:19). Jesus delighted to fulfill the Messianic prophesies found in the Old Testament.

> This was His work. He went about doing good and healing all that were oppressed by Satan. There were whole villages where there was not a moan of sickness in any house, for He had passed through them and healed all their sick. His work gave evidence of His divine anointing. Love, mercy, and compassion were revealed in every act of His life; His heart went out in tender sympathy to the children of men. He took man's nature, that He might reach man's wants. The poorest and humblest were not afraid to approach Him.

Even little children were attracted to Him. They loved to climb upon His knees and gaze into the pensive face, benignant with love.

. . . His life was one of self-denial and thoughtful care for others. Every soul was precious in His eyes. While He ever bore Himself with divine dignity, He bowed with the tenderest regard to every member of the family of God. In all men He saw fallen souls whom it was His mission to save.[1]

Of Jesus' innumerable miracles, His seven Sabbath miracles are described in detail in the Gospels. Five of them can be found in Matthew, Mark, and Luke, and two in the Gospel of John. To put these seven miracles in context, we must recall that Jewish law at the time allowed the "work" of caring for the critically ill if necessary to save a life. However, care for a person with a chronic condition would be classified as "work" and must wait until after Sabbath—as reviewed in the previous chapter. None of the seven recorded miracles Jesus performed on Sabbath were critical illnesses. Thus, according to Jewish law, no treatment or help should have been expected or given on the Sabbath:

- a demon-possessed man (Luke 4:31–37)
- Peter's mother-in-law with a high fever (Luke 4:38, 39)
- a man with a withered hand (Luke 6:6–11)
- a woman who had suffered with a crippled back for eighteen years (Luke 13:10–17)
- a man with dropsy (Luke 14:1–6)
- a man at the pool of Bethesda who had been ill for thirty-eight years (John 5:1–15)
- a man born blind (John 9)

None of those healed on the Sabbath came to Jesus begging to be healed, as often was the case with the sick on other days of the week. Of course, the Sabbath rules of the time likely were the reason. Because of this, Jesus' initiative in these Sabbath miracles is all the more striking.

For example, He healed some on Sabbath morning as He was teaching in the synagogue filled with Sabbath worshipers—such as the demon-possessed man, the man with a withered hand, and the woman with the crippled back. He would interrupt the service by calling the infirm person to the front so that everyone could see what He was going to do, rather than asking the person to meet Him privately after the service to spare Himself a lot of trouble.

Two other times, He deliberately sent the healed person into the heart of the city of Jerusalem on a Sabbath:

- He told the man at the pool of Bethesda to carry his bed— which would be obvious Sabbath breaking since carrying anything on the Sabbath was forbidden. This particular Sabbath was during one of the Jewish feasts, ("After this there was a feast of the Jews, and Jesus went up to Jerusalem" [John 5:1]) meaning Jerusalem would have been especially full of worshipers. The miracle would have been seen by even more people because they were in Jerusalem for the feast. Then, instead of being relieved that no one had seen this Sabbath miracle, sparing Him much angry antagonism, Jesus told the long-suffering man to carry his bed, deliberately positioning the miracle in public view.
- A blind man was told by Jesus to wash in the pool of Siloam, right near the temple. This would obviously make the miracle more public (John 9:6, 7).

Moreover, healing the man born blind found Jesus "breaking" several Sabbath laws of the time:

- He "spat on the ground"—irrigating was forbidden.

- He "made clay" with the soil—plowing was forbidden.
- He "anointed the eyes of the blind man"—applying medicine to a chronic condition was forbidden.
- He told the man to "wash in the pool of Siloam"—bathing also was forbidden.

When the man obeyed, the miracle became public, for no one would dare wash on Sabbath—especially in the pool by the temple.

Instead of celebrating these mighty acts of healing as fulfilling the long-anticipated Messianic miracles, the Jewish leaders continually accused Jesus of breaking the Sabbath, even insisting that He could not possibly be the Messiah because of this. Though they had long treasured the prophecies of the promised Messiah because of all the great acts He would do, they refused to accept the Sabbath miracles of Jesus as fulfilling prophecy. For example, in Mark's and Luke's records of Jesus healing the demon-possessed man on Sabbath (Mark 1:21–28; Luke 4:31–37), the people recognized the miracle as a supernatural act. Yet the religious leaders refused to admit that Jesus was fulfilling the Messianic prophecy of "proclaiming liberty to the captives." Instead, they bitterly excoriated Jesus for breaking the Sabbath.

When Jesus healed a woman's crippled back in the synagogue one Sabbath, the "presiding elder" sneered to the crowd because of the miracle: "There are six days on which men ought to work; therefore come and be healed on them, and not on the Sabbath day" (Luke 13:14). He scorned the miracle as "work" because current Sabbath restrictions forbade treating anyone's chronic condition. In their thinking, there was simply no possible reason for Jesus to "desecrate" the Sabbath this way. Having endured a crippled back for eighteen years, the woman could surely wait one more day, they reasoned. Their Sabbath rules must be obeyed.

For Jesus, however, Sabbath was a day to save people. He wanted to restore the link between Sabbath and life-giving salvation by deliberately healing chronic conditions as test cases. What is more, His defense of Sabbath healings underscored that He was the true Interpreter of the Sabbath. He insisted on His Messianic position by claiming the divine prerogative: "My Father has been working until now, and I have been working" (John 5:17). His choice of words about His Father and "working" added fuel to the fire! Now His accusers condemned Jesus not only for breaking the Sabbath but also for identifying Himself as divine (verse 18).

Preoccupation with Sabbath-keeping rules caused the divine intent of Sabbath as a day for healing and restoration to be lost. It is true that the Pharisees rightly understood the keeping of the Sabbath as a vital issue, but they had forgotten that keeping the Sabbath is meant to put one in position to be blessed and restored by the Lord of the Sabbath. Ellen White's reflections are rich:

The demands upon God are even greater upon the Sabbath than upon other days. His people then leave their usual employment, and spend the time in meditation and worship. They ask more favors of Him on the Sabbath than upon other days. They demand His special attention. They crave His choicest blessings. God does not wait for the Sabbath to pass before He grants these requests. Heaven's work never ceases, and men should never rest from doing good. The Sabbath is not intended to be a period of useless inactivity. The law forbids secular labor on the rest day of the Lord; the toil that gains a livelihood must cease; no labor for worldly pleasure or profit is lawful upon that day; but as God ceased His labor of creating, and rested upon the Sabbath and blessed it, so man is to leave the occupations of his daily life, and devote those sacred hours to healthful rest, to worship, and to holy deeds. The work of Christ in healing the sick was in perfect accord with the law. It honored the Sabbath.[2]

Rediscovering the Glory the Sabbath

The seven Sabbath miracles of Jesus provide valuable lessons:

- Jesus sought to restore the Sabbath's blessing and honor at the risk of His life. All four Gospel writers saw this and regularly drew attention to it. In addition to His seven Sabbath miracles, at least one chapter in every eight refers to the Sabbath—and sometimes at great length.
- Jesus defined what was "lawful" to do on the Sabbath— not by defending observance on the seventh day, for that wasn't an issue then. He based His teaching on the Old Testament—Moses and the prophets—and He instructed by His example.
- Jesus extended His invitation: "Come to Me, all you who labor and are heavy laden, and I will give you rest. Take My yoke upon you and learn from Me, for I am gentle and lowly in heart, and you will find rest for your souls. For My yoke is easy and My burden is light" (Matthew 11:28–30).

Matthew immediately connected this divine invitation to a narrative about a Sabbath controversy between Jesus and some of the religious leaders: "At that time Jesus went through the grain-fields on the Sabbath. And His disciples were hungry, and began to pluck heads of grain and to eat." When the Pharisees, who just happened to be in the field too, saw this, they complained to Jesus, "Look, Your disciples are doing what is not lawful to do on the Sabbath!" (Matthew 12:1, 2).

This was not a matter of the disciples unlawfully gleaning in someone else's field; the Torah permitted this: "When you come into your neighbor's standing grain, you may pluck the heads with your hand, but you shall not use a sickle on your neighbor's standing grain" (Deuteronomy 23:25). The issue was that the disciples were doing this on the Sabbath. Their action was especially suspect because picking grain (considered "harvesting") and rubbing the grain kernels in their hands (considered "threshing") were forbidden on the Sabbath. This kind of "work" was only allowed on weekdays.

Jesus didn't issue an immediate "no, you're wrong." Instead, He tried to uncover the Sabbath's depth of meaning that the Pharisees either hadn't seen or had ignored. Twice, Jesus gently inquired, "Have you not read?" (verses 3–8). He knew they had studied the Old Testament rigorously. But Jesus used the occasion to urge them to study for a deeper understanding. He was fully aware they knew the syntax and grammar of the Hebrew language—but they had missed the profound meanings of the Old Testament. He explained that requiring the disciples to deny their physical needs in order to keep the Sabbath would pervert its intended function as a day of delight!

The temple and the Sabbath were the two most sacred institutions for the Jews, and Jesus boldly declared Lordship over both. He declared that He was "Lord of the Sabbath" (Luke 6:5). And at another time, He said, "In this place there is One greater than the temple" (Matthew 12:6)—another Messianic claim! Jesus sought to remind the Jews that both the Sabbath and the temple services were to be blessings, not burdensome requirements. He attempted to take their thinking to a deeper level. These statements of Jesus should be given careful attention by anyone who truly seeks to understand what the Creator intended the Sabbath to be and what it means to keep it holy.

When performing His seven Sabbath miracles, Jesus did nothing to avoid controversy. He took the initiative and did the miracles publicly, setting up the scene so the miracle would not be hidden—either on Sabbath morning in the synagogue service or by sending the healed person out into public view. The religious leaders had so warped Sabbath truth that even their religiosity was faulty, as Ellen White comments:

The Saviour well knew that in healing on the Sabbath He would be regarded as a transgressor, but He did not hesitate to break down the wall of traditional requirements that barricaded the Sabbath. . . .

. . . Every false religion teaches its adherents to be careless of human needs, sufferings, and rights. The gospel places a high value upon humanity as the purchase of the blood of Christ, and it teaches a tender regard for the wants and woes of man.[3]

Jesus didn't challenge traditional Sabbath rules for leading camels or making knots. Instead, He sought to restore the true meaning of the Sabbath as a day of salvation, for making people whole again. The real issue for the religious leaders was accepting the "Lord of the Sabbath." He created it and, in the Old Testament, called it "My holy day" (Isaiah 58:13). And throughout His earthly ministry, Jesus insisted He was the true interpreter of it—and the provider of Sabbath rest and healing. He ever sought to get to the "heart of the matter"!

Notably, as Jesus interpreted the Sabbath's meaning, He was also inferring the perpetual nature of the Decalogue—of which the Sabbath commandment is the longest. This can be seen in His preaching ministry, especially in His long-treasured sermon on the mount. However, people mostly refer to the Beatitudes without continuing to His commentary on the Decalogue. There, He called attention to the expansive parameters of the commandments (Matthew 5:13–32)—and how these commandments would make His followers both "salt" and a "light" in the world, implying that the Sabbath would be part of this blessing.

When foretelling the future in Matthew 24, Jesus spoke of the Sabbath, which meant it would be continuing (Matthew 24:20).

Luke closes his account of Christ's earthly ministry by reporting that His crucified body was placed in the tomb of a believing Pharisee, Joseph of Arimathea, late on a Friday afternoon—as

The Lord of the Sabbath: His Day and His Disciples

"the Sabbath drew near." As Jesus rested on the Sabbath upon completing His work of creation, He now rested on the Sabbath after completing His work of salvation. In fact, within seven verses, Luke refers to preparation as the Sabbath drew near and the women resting on the seventh-day Sabbath during Crucifixion weekend, and he verifies that Sunday was the day of the Resurrection:

Now behold, there was a man named Joseph, a council member, a good and just man. He had not consented to their decision and deed. He was from Arimathea, a city of the Jews, who himself was also waiting for the kingdom of God. This man went to Pilate and asked for the body of Jesus. Then he took it down, wrapped it in linen, and laid it in a tomb that was hewn out of the rock, where no one had ever lain before. *That day was the Preparation, and the Sabbath drew near.*

And the women who had come with Him from Galilee followed after, and they observed the tomb and how His body was laid. Then they returned and prepared spices and fragrant oils. And *they rested on the Sabbath according to the commandment.**

Now on the first day of the week, very early in the morning, they, and certain other women with them, came to the tomb bringing the spices which they had prepared (Luke 23:50–24:1; emphasis added).

These verses in no way imply that the Sabbath would be changing because of Resurrection Sunday. Rather, they substantiate the continuing seven-day week by affirming the Sabbath as part of the commandments.

Jesus, whose birth was miraculous, and who was willing to die for the sins of the world—this same Jesus

---

* The account continues directly to chapter 24. Chapter divisions are not original and must not be allowed to make a break in the narrative flow.

- created the Sabbath,
- blessed the Sabbath,
- sanctified the Sabbath,
- worshiped on the Sabbath,
- rested on the Sabbath after completing the work of salvation as He had done after completing the work of Creation, and
- declared Himself "Lord of the Sabbath."

All this He did to extol the extraordinary nature of His holy day, for it is

- a memorial of Creation,
- a symbol of Redemption,
- a sign of sanctification,
- the seal of the covenant, and
- established forever as part of eternal worship (Isaiah 66:22, 23).

Jesus was Jewish, all the writers of the New Testament were Jewish except for Luke, and the apostles were Jewish. The Sabbath, however, is not Jewish. It was gifted to humankind before there was a Jew and even before sin. And though the Jewish people have been keeping the seventh-day Sabbath for thousands of years, the Sabbath is never called "Jewish" in the Bible. It was created thousands of years before there were any Jews! In Mark 2:27, Jesus stated that the Sabbath was made for *man*, not for any people group. And when sin is finally removed and destroyed from this earth, we will still be celebrating the blessed Sabbath!

Might it be today that some Sabbath keepers are still misunderstanding what the Sabbath is all about—thinking it is legislation to be obeyed rather than a day to celebrate the grace of God and the healing He longs to bestow? We must not be satisfied with trusting our performance of the forms of religion and lose touch with the Lord of the Sabbath. Instead, each Sabbath, we should see ourselves as needing the healing that only Jesus can bring—restoring our spiritual eyesight and healing our crippled moral backbones—and participate in the healing power of His touch. He has never been fooled with our pretentious piety and pseudo ritualism, and He yearns to give us rest in His salvific healing.

Sabbath in the book of Acts

Though a large percentage of the New Testament was written by the apostle Paul to the new churches he established and to a few pastors, the other major contributor to the New Testament corpus was the Gentile Luke, whom Paul refers to as "Luke the beloved physician" (Colossians 4:14). He wrote one large book, now separated into two: his Gospel and the book of Acts. In both, Luke manifested a major interest in the Sabbath. In his Gospel, he reports five of Jesus' Sabbath miracles, along with other references to the Sabbath.

In his book The Acts of the Apostles, Luke continues to document the first-century Christian church (Acts 15:21; 16:13; 17:1, 2; 18:4), showing its dynamic growth through the impressive cross-cultural ministry of Paul. And, as might be expected because of Luke's focus on the Sabbath in his Gospel, the Sabbath again figures large in Acts. He writes about it several times.

For example, in Acts 4, Peter and John are arrested for their Christ-centered preaching: "Now as they spoke to the people, the priests, the captain of the temple, and the Sadducees came upon them, being greatly disturbed that they taught the people and preached in Jesus the resurrection from the dead. And they laid hands on them, and put them in custody until the next day, for it was already evening" (Acts 4:1–3).

The next day Peter and John were interrogated by an impressive "court," including "rulers, elders, and scribes, as well as Annas, the high priest, Caiaphas, John, and Alexander, and as many as were of the family of the high priest," who "were gathered together at Jerusalem" (verses 5, 6). When Peter and John boldly defended Jesus, it unnerved the high court. So they decided to "severely threaten them, that from now on they speak to no man in this name" (verse 17). Peter and John remained brave apologists and defended their motive for ministry. Again, the court threatened them but let them go, realizing that the people's respect for Peter and John was strong.

Being let go, the two preachers returned to their friends and reported what had happened—and they all raised their voices in praise "with one accord and said: 'Lord, You are God, who *made heaven and earth and the sea, and all that is in them*' " (verse 24; emphasis added). Their prayer, in which they praised the mighty God, opened with this quote from the fourth commandment of the Decalogue! This is a remarkable recognition of the Creator, the Lord of the Sabbath!

This happens again on a later occasion, as we will see. But before that, in Acts 13, we read what Luke wrote about one of Paul's journeys into the Gentile territory: "When they departed from Perga, they came to Antioch in Pisidia, and went into the synagogue on the Sabbath day and sat down. And after the reading of the Law and the Prophets, the rulers of the synagogue sent to them, saying, 'Men and brethren, if you have any word of exhortation for the people, say on' " (verses 14, 15).

Though in Gentile territory, Paul continued keeping the Sabbath—joining worship in a synagogue. When invited to give a "word of exhortation," Paul gave a lengthy sermon about Jesus, which Luke included. It should be noticed that in the book of Acts, Paul did a lot of preaching—but sermon content is not always recorded. This sermon in Antioch of Pisidia is. It contains a rich defense of Christ, which many of Paul's own people had rejected "because they did not know Him, nor even the voices of the Prophets which are read every Sabbath" (verse 27).

The Lord of the Sabbath: His Day and His Disciples

At the end of the service, notice what happened. "When the Jews went out of the synagogue, *the Gentiles begged that these words might be preached to them the next Sabbath.* Now when the congregation had broken up, many of the Jews and devout proselytes followed Paul and Barnabas, who, speaking to them, persuaded them to continue in the grace of God" (verses 42, 43; emphasis added).

Apparently, Jews and Gentiles were worshiping together that Sabbath morning in the synagogue. And it was the Gentiles who begged that Paul preach again on "the next Sabbath." Paul then encouraged the "Jews and devout proselytes" to continue in God's grace. The preaching invitation was obviously welcomed, for "on the next Sabbath almost the whole city came together to hear the word of God" (verse 44).

These narratives give no indication that the first-century church was tending toward worshiping on Sunday in honor of the Resurrection, even though Paul was certainly preaching about the resurrection of Jesus. Moreover, nowhere in the book of Acts was Paul ever accused of breaking the Sabbath—nor did he even subtly hint that Sunday sacredness was starting. Paul was harshly condemned for not insisting that new Gentile converts be circumcised, but he was never accused of tampering with Sabbath sacredness all through his many missionary journeys.

The "Judaizers" kept accusing Paul when it came to the long-standing Jewish practice of circumcision, for Paul was openly adamant against the necessity of it for Gentile Christians. But the Judaizers never accused Paul of breaking the Sabbath or seeking to change it. This crucial point needs to be emphasized when seeking to understand the historical background of Sunday sacredness in the Christian church.

On another occasion, when Paul and Barnabas were preaching in Lystra, a crippled man was among those listening, and "Paul, observing him intently and seeing that he had faith to be healed, said with a loud voice, 'Stand up straight on your feet!' And he leaped and walked" (Acts 14:9, 10). This was so impressive and rightly recognized by the people in this Gentile city as a divine miracle that they immediately wanted to worship Paul and Barnabas. Even the priest of Zeus came prepared to offer sacrifices to them.

But when the apostles Barnabas and Paul heard this, they tore their clothes and ran in among the multitude, crying out and saying, "Men, why are you doing these things? We also are men with the same nature as you, and preach to you that you should turn from these useless things to *the living God, who made the heaven, the earth, the sea, and all things that are in them,* who in bygone generations allowed all nations to walk in their own ways. Nevertheless He did not leave Himself without witness, in that He *did good,* gave us rain from heaven and fruitful seasons, filling our hearts with food and gladness" (verses 14–17; emphasis added).

Again, with a direct quote from the fourth commandment of the Decalogue, Paul identified the true God with His own words! His "good" creation is also included in their defense. But, even so, they could "scarcely restrain the multitudes from sacrificing to them" (verse 18), so powerful was the healing miracle to those in Lystra who saw it.

In Acts 16, mention is made of Paul's visit to Philippi, a prominent city in Macedonia, and how he spent the Sabbath there:

Therefore, sailing from Troas, we ran a straight course to Samothrace, and the next day came to Neapolis, and from there to Philippi, which is the foremost city of that part of Macedonia, a colony. And we were staying in that city for some days. And *on the Sabbath day we went out of the city to the riverside, where prayer was customarily made*; and we sat down and spoke to the women who met there. Now a certain woman named Lydia heard us. She was a seller of purple from the city of Thyatira, who worshiped God. The Lord opened her heart to heed the things spoken by Paul. And when she and her household were baptized, she begged us, saying, "If you have judged me to be faithful to the Lord, come to my house and stay." So she persuaded us (verses 11–15; emphasis added).

Christians were not allowed to build churches at this time; thus, they often met in homes—or, in this case, outside the city by the river. Again, there is no indication that Sabbath sacredness on the seventh day was shifting to another day.

Acts 17 finds Paul again worshiping on the seventh-day Sabbath in another Gentile city: "Now when they had passed through Amphipolis and Apollonia, they came to Thessalonica, where there was a synagogue of the Jews. Then *Paul, as his custom was, went in to them, and for three Sabbaths reasoned with them from the Scriptures,* explaining and demonstrating that the Christ had to suffer and rise again from the dead, and saying, 'This Jesus whom I preach to you is the Christ.' And some of them were persuaded; and a great multitude of the devout Greeks, and not a few of the leading women, joined Paul and Silas" (verses 1–4; emphasis added).

No mention is made of Paul defending the seventh-day Sabbath all through the book of Acts. He didn't need to because it wasn't an issue. Rather, he kept championing the truth about Jesus, which *was* an issue. And in this case, Luke described Paul's Sabbath customs the same way he had described Jesus' Sabbath keeping: "as his custom was" (Luke 4:16; Acts 17:2).

Paul traveled to Corinth and settled there for a while. In that city, again, his Sabbath customs are cited: "Paul departed from Athens and went to Corinth. And he found a certain Jew named

Aquila, born in Pontus, who had recently come from Italy with his wife Priscilla (because Claudius had commanded all the Jews to depart from Rome); and he came to them. So, because he was of the same trade, he stayed with them and worked; for by occupation they were tentmakers. *And he reasoned in the synagogue every Sabbath, and persuaded both Jews and Greeks*" (Acts 18:1–4, emphasis added).

Paul ever worshiped on the seventh-day Sabbath. And apparently, both Jews and Gentiles were worshiping together on Sabbath and listening to Paul. He wasn't seeking to change anyone's mind about which day was the Sabbath. He merely continued to worship on the seventh day and uphold the law.

Paul and the law—including the Sabbath

The great apostle who wrote much of the New Testament materials did not spend time defending the seventh day as the Sabbath or even calling attention to it. But it must be remembered that, in his letters, he didn't bother to address theological doctrines or topics that weren't problems in the churches he founded. He is called a "contextual" theologian because of the way he dealt with the issues troubling new converts in their specific contexts. This does not mean that Paul did not keep the Sabbath or was subtly preparing the way for the first day of the week to increase in importance. Rather, in the book of Acts, we have seen that he kept Sabbath along with the new Gentile Christians.

There is no indication in the book of Acts or in any of Paul's letters that suggests that Gentile Christians were worshiping on a different day by themselves. The new Gentile Christians were keeping the seventh-day Sabbath, and thus there was no need for Paul to explain and defend it further. Apparently, he had so carefully instructed the new Christian converts about the Sabbath that there was no raging controversy regarding it as there was over the issue of circumcision.

The Lord of the Sabbath: His Day and His Disciples

Paul also emphatically urged believers not to depart from what he had taught them: "But even if we, or an angel from heaven, preach any other gospel to you than what we have preached to you, let him be accursed" (Galatians 1:8). The book of Acts describes him spending much time teaching and carefully instructing new Christian converts as he established churches in different cities. Moreover, he never hesitated to confront false teaching and urged the importance of "sound doctrine" (see Titus 1:9; 2:1; 1 Timothy 1:10; 2 Timothy 4:3).

Though Paul rarely referred to the fourth commandment, he did quote some of the other commandments in the Decalogue, indicating that the law was still the standard of holiness (for example, Romans 7:7, 8; Romans 13:9). In a couple of passages, some think that Paul implied that the law was not necessary because of Jesus' death. And on this basis, they believe that Christians are relieved of the burden of the law. However, Paul strongly insists in his lengthy letter to the Romans that the law is not void: "Do we then make void the law through faith? Certainly not! On the contrary, we establish the law" (Romans 3:31). This is a critical point.

Furthermore, without the law, there is no need for grace! What Paul condemns is the idea that one *can be saved* by keeping the law. And that is a critical point too. If anyone is going to be saved, it will be by grace because even our best obedience comes through our corrupt human channels. The prophet Isaiah also taught this in the Old Testament:

But we are all like an unclean thing,
And all our righteousnesses are like filthy rags;
We all fade as a leaf,
And our iniquities, like the wind,
Have taken us away (Isaiah 64:6).

The epistle to the Hebrews

Though there is debate about the authorship of Hebrews, one is not out on a limb in suggesting it was Paul. The grammar, writing style, and energy are "Pauline." True, there are differences in style and content between the book of Hebrews and Paul's other writings. And the book does not contain Paul's customary "signature" usually found in his other letters. However, such considerations need not completely dismiss Paul's authorship—for the book of Hebrews is the only letter that he writes to his own people. Therefore, he freely cites the Old Testament in it more than any of his other letters. His people had grown up with the Old Testament. All his other letters are written to churches he established in prominent Gentile cities and whose Gentile converts caused quite a (negative) stir among the Jewish Christians in Jerusalem. These new believers would not have had the opportunity to be as familiar with the Old Testament as their fellow Jewish believers would have.

Moreover, at this time, apparently, Christians were suffering from major persecution. Paul, more than once, was constrained to urge his Jewish people not to give up their faith in Jesus: "Therefore we must give the more earnest heed to the things we have heard, lest we drift away. For if the word spoken through angels proved steadfast, and every transgression and disobedience received a just reward, how shall we escape if we neglect so great a salvation, which at the first began to be spoken by the Lord, and was confirmed to us by those who heard Him, God also bearing witness both with signs and wonders, with various miracles, and gifts of the Holy Spirit, according to His own will?" (Hebrews 2:1–4).

But recall the former days in which, after you were illuminated, you endured a great struggle with sufferings: partly while you were made a spectacle both by reproaches and tribulations, and partly while you became companions of those who were so treated; for you had compassion on me in my chains, and joyfully accepted the plundering of your goods, knowing that you have a better and an enduring possession for yourselves in heaven. Therefore do not cast away your confidence, which has great reward. For you have need of endurance, so that after you have done the will of God, you may receive the promise:

"For yet a little while,
And He who is coming will come and will not tarry.
Now the just shall live by faith;
But if anyone draws back,
My soul has no pleasure in him."

But we are not of those who draw back to perdition, but of those who believe to the saving of the soul (Hebrews 10:32–39).

Doubt and disbelief often arise in the face of severe persecution. And just as in the rest of the New Testament, believers are urged not to lose their faith. The general letters and epistles were not written to convert pagans, but rather to bolster the faith of new believers. The writers (Paul, along with Luke, Peter, and John) were also addressing the various situations at hand. Seventh-day Adventists face a similar situation. While still urging the second coming of Jesus, faith must be encouraged in the face of long years of waiting and many giving up their hope.

The Epistle to the Hebrews is a major composition that some call Paul's magnum opus. In its thirteen chapters, the writer demonstrated great proficiency in the Greek language. The content skillfully weaves together several major issues while appealing to the Hebrews to hold fast their belief in Jesus. In his detailed discourse, he discusses the Sabbath in chapter four, providing an extremely important summary of Sabbath doctrine.

First, in Hebrews 1, Paul instructs how the Old Testament is still normative for New Testament Christians—the inspired norm for truth and ethics. He writes, "God, who at various times and in various ways spoke in time past to the fathers by the prophets, has in these last days spoken to us by His Son, whom He has appointed heir of all things, through whom also He made the worlds" (Hebrews 1:1, 2).

Jesus is not in opposition to the Old Testament because the same God is the Author of both. The Sabbath is upheld as a distinctive aspect of faith. Because Jesus is now High Priest, much of the Old Testament system of faith is replaced/fulfilled in Jesus—but not the Sabbath! It remains. Neither Jesus nor Paul were innovators. Rather, they took up all the prophecies, types, and symbols embedded in the Old Testament and demonstrated their fulfillment in Jesus. All pointed to Him and His great salvific mission. The Sabbath is not prophetic. It is not symbolic. It is not Jewish. It is just what is written about it: a memorial of Creation, the sign of salvation, and a promise for rest.

In Hebrews 4, Sabbath rest is linked to the original Sabbath of the very first week during Creation:

Therefore, since a promise remains of entering His rest, let us fear lest any of you seem to have come short of it. For indeed the gospel was preached to us as well as to them; but the word which they heard did not profit them, not being mixed with faith in those who heard it. For we who have believed do enter that rest, as He has said:

"So I swore in My wrath,
'They shall not enter My rest,' "

although the works were finished from the foundation of the

world. For He has spoken in a certain place of the seventh day in this way: "And God rested on the seventh day from all His works" (verses 1–4).

The last sentence refers to Genesis 2, thereby manifesting its bond or connection with the seventh-day Sabbath and rest in Jesus. God's rest for humanity is not only rest from sin and guilt but also a rest needed from the beginning, even before sin entered!

Creation and Redemption are unbreakably, tightly linked in all of God's work. God has not been experimenting, nor did He need to think up a new plan:

- "For we who have believed do enter that rest, . . . although *the works were finished from the foundation of the world*" (Hebrews 4:3; emphasis added).
- "Then the King will say to those on His right hand, 'Come, you blessed of My Father, inherit *the kingdom prepared for you from the foundation of the world*'" (Matthew 25:34; emphasis added).
- "All who dwell on the earth will worship him, whose names have not been written in the Book of Life of *the Lamb slain from the foundation of the world*" (Revelation 13:8; emphasis added).

Hebrews 8 again reminds the reader of the rest for God's people that Christ's redemption provides: "Now this is the main point of the things we are saying: We have such a High Priest, who is seated at the right hand of the throne of the Majesty in the heavens, a Minister of the sanctuary and of the true tabernacle which the Lord erected, and not man" (Hebrews 8:1, 2).

We have been promised rest through Jesus, our High Priest— the Mediator of God's rest for our souls. God's rest on that first seventh day, during Creation week, becomes the foundation for all Sabbath theology, with an unbroken continuity unfolding throughout Scripture:

Creation –> Israel –> New Testament church –>
Jesus' second coming –> heaven

"For this is the covenant that I will make with the house of Israel after those days, says the LORD: I will put My laws in their mind and write them on their hearts; and I will be their God, and they shall be My people. None of them shall teach his neighbor, and none his brother, saying, 'Know the LORD,' for all shall know Me, from the least of them to the greatest of them. For I will be merciful to their unrighteousness, and their sins and their lawless deeds I will remember no more" (verses 10–12).

The Sabbath commandment, in the heart of the Decalogue and containing a third of its words, is distinct and separate from the bloody sacrifices that Christ fulfilled with His great sacrifice. Sabbath rest, given at the beginning, will last through eternity:

"For as the new heavens and the new earth
Which I will make shall remain before Me," says the LORD,
"So shall your descendants and your name remain.
And it shall come to pass
That from one New Moon to another,
And from one Sabbath to another,
All flesh shall come to worship before Me," says the LORD
    (Isaiah 66:22, 23).

The Sabbath was never meant to be for any one people group. Notice: when God called Abraham, it was so he could be a blessing to the whole world:

The Lord of the Sabbath: His Day and His Disciples

Now the LORD had said to Abram:

> "Get out of your country,
> From your family
> And from your father's house,
> To a land that I will show you.
> I will make you a great nation;
> I will bless you
> And make your name great;
> And *you shall be a blessing.*
> I will bless those who bless you,
> And I will curse him who curses you;
> And *in you all the families of the earth shall be blessed*"
> (Genesis 12:1–3; emphasis added).

And later, when God bestowed the covenant blessings on Isaac, He spoke of Abraham's obedience:

> Then the LORD appeared to him and said: "Do not go down to Egypt; live in the land of which I shall tell you. Dwell in this land, and I will be with you and bless you; for to you and your descendants I give all these lands, and I will perform the oath which I swore to Abraham your father. And I will make your descendants multiply as the stars of heaven; I will give to your descendants all these lands; and *in your seed all the nations of the earth shall be blessed; because Abraham obeyed My voice and kept My charge, My commandments, My statutes, and My laws*" (Genesis 26:2–5; emphasis added).

Obeying the law was never meant to be a way of earning salvation but was to be the means of blessing others! Sabbath rest is part of the divine blessing. Think of it: when Sabbath keepers don't understand or share the glories of Sabbath rest, God's blessings are stifled!

Rediscovering the Glory the Sabbath

The parameters of the Sabbath are vast, including future eschatological fulfillment. The Sabbath includes assurance of future glory, in which God invites all nations and peoples to participate. In the meantime, there is Sabbath rest:

> For if Joshua had given them rest, then He would not afterward have spoken of another day. *There remains therefore a rest for the people of God.* For he who has entered His rest has himself also ceased from his works as God did from His.
> *Let us therefore be diligent to enter that rest* (Hebrews 4:8–11; emphasis added).

A rest "remains" for the people of God. This is a rest from our works, as God rested from His that first Sabbath. For us, it keeps us from thinking we have to work seven days a week and helps us realize that the world will survive without our incessant labor. It especially teaches us to rest in God's work of salvation, which we could never earn by ourselves.

There are, in fact, "labors" of disobedience and unbelief that can prevent us from entering God's rest. The Jewish religious leaders in Christ's day strictly observed the seventh day, but their hearts were filled with hatred for Jesus. They had never learned to accept God's "rest" and to cease from relying on their own works. They had no excuse because the Old Testament had already warned them:

> Thus says the LORD:
>
> > "Stand in the ways and see,
> > And *ask for the old paths, where the good way is,*
> > *And walk in it;*
> > *Then you will find rest for your souls.*
> > But they said, 'We will not walk in it' " (Jeremiah 6:16; emphasis added).

The Lord of the Sabbath: His Day and His Disciples

Acknowledging the seventh day as Sabbath is important, but it isn't enough. God Himself distinguished the seventh day from the other six days and upheld this distinction in the fourth commandment. He is clear: six days are for work with the next day for rest.

But we are not on our own for six days! Acknowledging the biblical Sabbath is acknowledging that *God is with us every day.* The divine Author of Sabbath commands rest, proving He is not a slave driver.

Hebrews 4 makes clear that God's Word is a living Word—a powerful, piercing sword:

> Let us therefore be diligent to enter that rest, lest anyone fall according to the same example of disobedience. *For the word of God is living and powerful, and sharper than any two-edged sword*, piercing even to the division of soul and spirit, and of joints and marrow, and is *a discerner of the thoughts and intents of the heart*. And there is no creature hidden from His sight, but all things are naked and open to the eyes of Him to whom we must give account (verses 11–13; emphasis added).

Chapter four climaxes with a "therefore": "Let us therefore come boldly to the throne of grace, that we may obtain mercy and find grace to help in time of need" (verse 16). This is an amazing picture of God. If we are invited to a "throne," that means we are dealing with a king. And if it is a "throne of grace," this divine King can never be accused of being unforgiving and harsh. He bids us come to His throne so that He can give us something. He is not asking something of us or taking something from us. This is a rare king!

What is more, we are not invited to ask modestly for just a little bit but to ask "boldly" for as much as our hearts can hold—for at the throne of this King, we can "obtain mercy and find grace to help in time of need."

Why do we need "mercy and grace"? We are implored to receive it because we are sinful:

- "The heart is deceitful above all things, and desperately wicked; who can know it?" (Jeremiah 17:9).
- "Who can understand his errors?
  Cleanse me from secret faults.
  Keep back Your servant also from presumptuous sins;
  Let them not have dominion over me.
  Then I shall be blameless,
  And I shall be innocent of great transgression" (Psalm 19:12, 13).

Ellen White also reminds, even our best efforts are polluted by sin,

> Christ, our Mediator, and the Holy Spirit are constantly interceding in man's behalf, but the Spirit pleads not for us as does Christ, who presents His blood, shed from the foundation of the world; the Spirit works upon our hearts, drawing out prayers and penitence, praise and thanksgiving. The gratitude which flows from our lips is the result of the Spirit's striking the cords of the soul in holy memories, awakening the music of the heart.
>
> The religious services, the prayers, the praise, the penitent confession of sin ascend from true believers as incense to the heavenly sanctuary, but passing through the corrupt channels of humanity, they are so defiled that unless purified by blood, they can never be of value with God. They ascend not in spotless purity, and unless the Intercessor, who is at God's right hand, presents and purifies all by His righteousness, it is not acceptable to God. All incense

from earthly tabernacles must be moist with the cleansing drops of the blood of Christ. He holds before the Father the censer of His own merits, in which there is no taint of earthly corruption. He gathers into this censer the prayers, the praise, and the confessions of His people, and with these He puts His own spotless righteousness. Then, perfumed with the merits of Christ's propitiation, the incense comes up before God wholly and entirely acceptable. Then gracious answers are returned.

Oh, that all may see that everything in obedience, in penitence, in praise and thanksgiving, must be placed upon the glowing fire of the righteousness of Christ. The fragrance of this righteousness ascends like a cloud around the mercy seat.[4]

The apostle Paul also wrote about this: "Likewise the Spirit also helps in our weaknesses. For we do not know what we should pray for as we ought, but the Spirit Himself makes intercession for us with groanings which cannot be uttered. Now He who searches the hearts knows what the mind of the Spirit is, because He makes intercession for the saints according to the will of God" (Romans 8:26, 27).

In Hebrews, his major tome to his own people, Paul was not writing to Sunday keepers but to the Hebrew people and thus did not need to prove that the seventh day was the Sabbath. However, he underscored its everlasting richness to Jewish believers who had accepted Christ as their Savior. Paul reminded them that the Sabbath was a divine gift before the Fall ("works were finished from the foundation of the world" [Hebrews 4:3]) and that it was maintained after the Fall because of its unchangeable nature. He even linked it with grace in Hebrews 4. Paul insisted that Sabbath rest is the rest of grace to God's people in all ages, acknowledging Jesus as the One who gives rest: "Come to Me, all you who labor and are heavy laden, and I will give you rest. Take My yoke upon you and learn from Me, for I am gentle and lowly in heart, and you will find rest for your souls. For My yoke is easy and My burden is light" (Matthew 11:28–30).

In the book of Hebrews, Paul identified three dimensions of the Sabbath:

- in the *past*: its historical origin, which completed the Creation week of seven literal days
- in the *present*: its present restorative, redeeming power for God's people (The bloody sacrifices were fulfilled in Jesus, but Sabbath rest remains.)
- in the *future*: anticipating the eternal rest of sinless perfection with Jesus

The Sabbath is a test of whether we accept or reject the gospel—and it reveals that we cannot obtain righteousness by our good works. Rather, as God declared in the Old Testament, it is a sign that He is making us holy! (See Exodus 31:13; Ezekiel 20:12, 19, 20.)

The biblical Sabbath has always been a divine gift. God yearns for everyone to participate in what He created so He can restore fallen humanity to fellowship with Himself. And entering into the rest of God every Sabbath means entering a rest of grace. This is not and, indeed, cannot be legalism!

Sabbath in the New Testament general epistles and letters

The books often called the general epistles were written by James, Peter, Jude, and John. Those seeking to establish Sunday sacredness sometimes point to the absence of the term *Sabbath* in the general epistles as evidence that the seventh-day Sabbath was already shifting to Sunday. The writers of the epistles don't address the fourth commandment of the Decalogue. They don't even mention the biblical Sabbath, let alone defend it.

However, this does not mean that the epistle writers no longer kept the Sabbath. Nor does it mean that Sabbath observance had changed or stopped. Peter and John were disciples of Jesus, while James and Jude were His half-brothers. They were leaders in the new Christian movement and are named in the Gospels and in the book of Acts (chapter 15). They were careful to defend various beliefs grounded in the Old Testament that were in danger of being lost or disobeyed—and they were adept at knowing how to present their defenses.

However, there is no evidence that there was a need to defend the seventh-day Sabbath. Being so well established and unquestioned, the doctrine was never a point of controversy. The writers simply did not need to defend the seventh day nor call for any shift in Sabbath's sacredness.

In the first century, "a great persecution arose against the church which was at Jerusalem; and they were all scattered throughout the regions of Judea and Samaria, except the apostles" (Acts 8:1). And Luke adds that, as the Christians fled Jerusalem, "those who were scattered went everywhere preaching the word" (verse 4). Apparently, they never let go of the Sabbath—and the issue of the seventh day being the Sabbath never needed defense.

The book of James

James, in chapter two of his epistle, makes a passing mention of worship in the synagogue (James 2:2).* He does not suggest that there was any problem with doing this. He does, however, reprove them for their unloving hearts toward the needy, even while gathered in the assembly. In connection with his admonition,

---

* The word translated "assembly" is the Greek word for *synagogue*, which means "assembly." James's use of *synagogue* suggests the scattered believers still faithfully went to synagogue worship on the Sabbath in the places where they were, as also mentioned in Acts 13:14; 16:13; 17:2; 18:4.

James refers to the Decalogue a few verses later, emphasizing its unchanging nature:

> If you really fulfill the royal law according to the Scripture, "You shall love your neighbor as yourself," you do well; but if you show partiality, you commit sin, and are convicted by the law as transgressors. For *whoever shall keep the whole law, and yet stumble in one point, he is guilty of all.* For He who said, "Do not commit adultery," also said, "Do not murder." Now if you do not commit adultery, but you do murder, you have become a transgressor of the law. So speak and so do as those who will be judged by the law of liberty (James 2:8–12; emphasis added).

Notably, the word *nomos* (law) is a key word in the epistle of James.* He instructs that those who are obedient to the law will be blessed: "He who looks into the perfect law of liberty and continues in it, and is not a forgetful hearer but a doer of the work, this one will be blessed in what he does" (James 1:25).

Several studies have noted the intertextual connection between the epistle of James and Jesus' sermon on the mount.[5] One of the prominent themes between them is the law—the Ten Commandments (James 1:25; 2:8–12; 4:11; Matthew 5:21, 22, 27, 28, 31–34, 38, 39). Jesus taught that the law is eternal, and not one commandment is allowed to be broken: "Do not think that I came to destroy the Law or the Prophets. I did not come to destroy but to fulfill. For assuredly, I say to you, till heaven and earth pass away, one jot or one tittle will by no means pass from the law till all is fulfilled. Whoever therefore breaks one of the least of these commandments, and teaches men so, shall be called least in the kingdom of heaven; but whoever does and teaches them, he shall

---

* In the book of James, the term *nomos* occurs ten times: James 1:25; 2:8, 9, 10, 11, 12; and four times in 4:11.

be called great in the kingdom of heaven" (Matthew 5:17–19). It is reasonable to think that the fourth commandment was included with the other nine that must still be obeyed. Jesus was not opening the door for a shift of days.

James addresses the Decalogue the same way, citing a couple of the commandments to infer the rest of them. He underscores his intention by the strong statement: "For whoever shall keep the whole law, and yet stumble in one point, he is guilty of all" (James 2:10). "All" refers to the entire Decalogue. Later in his letter, James wrote explicitly about several of the commandments:

- "But if you have bitter envy and self-seeking in your hearts, do not boast and *lie* against the truth" (James 3:14; emphasis added).
- "Where do wars and fights come from among you? Do they not come from your desires for pleasure that war in your members? You lust and do not have. You *murder* and *covet* and cannot obtain" (James 4:1, 2; emphasis added).
- "*Adulterers and adulteresses!* Do you not know that friendship with the world is enmity with God?" (verse 4; emphasis added).
- "There is one Lawgiver, who is able to save and to destroy. Who are you to judge another?" (verse 12).

Prohibitions against adultery and murder are found both in the Old Testament Decalogue and in Jesus' sermon on the mount. By mentioning a few of the Ten Commandments, both Jesus and James are implicitly referring to the entire Decalogue while they explicitly argue that the entire law must be kept—that obeying only a few of the commandments would not suffice. It can hardly be suggested that the Sabbath commandment was being excluded, ignored, or changed.

Although the word *Sabbath* is not used, the message of the

Sabbath is certainly implied by both James and Jesus. The inseparable unity of the Decalogue as an indivisible whole is clear—each of the Ten Commandments is equal in importance. The Sabbath commandment, the most substantial of the ten, can hardly be changed or disregarded!

The two letters of Peter

While the word *Sabbath* does not appear in the epistles of Peter, the word *commandment*, with specific reference to the Decalogue, does. Peter described false teachers "having eyes full of *adultery* and that cannot cease from sin, enticing unstable souls. They have a heart trained in *covetous* practices, and are accursed children. They have forsaken the right way and gone astray" (2 Peter 2:14, 15; emphasis added). "For if, after they have escaped the pollutions of the world through the knowledge of the Lord and Savior Jesus Christ, they are again entangled in them and overcome, the latter end is worse for them than the beginning. For it would have been better for them not to have known the way of righteousness, than having known it, to *turn from the holy commandment delivered to them*" (verses 20, 21; emphasis added).

Just as Jesus, Paul, and James, Peter refers to the whole Decalogue by mentioning only a few of the commandments. He also mentions "lawlessness" in referring to Sodom and Gomorrah. God, "turning the cities of Sodom and Gomorrah into ashes, condemned them to destruction, making them an example to those who afterward would live ungodly; and delivered righteous Lot, who was oppressed by the filthy conduct of the wicked (for that righteous man, dwelling among them, tormented his righteous soul from day to day by seeing and hearing their *lawless deeds*)" (verses 6–8; emphasis added).

The third chapter of Second Peter mentions the great acts of God: Creation (verse 5); the Flood (verse 6); Redemption (verse 10); the Second Coming (verses 3, 4, 10–12); and the promised new heaven and new earth (verse 13). The true Sabbath plays a major role in these events: Creation, the Flood (the weekly cycle is referred to several times), Jesus' seven Sabbath miracles of salvation, and the promised new heaven and new earth, where Sabbath will still be celebrated (Isaiah 66:22, 23).

The epistles of John

The word *commandment* appears in John's writings more than anywhere else in the New Testament. The pairing of the plural noun *commandments* with the verb *to keep* is used ten times in the New Testament. Eight of these are from the pen of John (John 14:15; 15:10; 1 John 2:3, 4; 3:22; 5:3; Revelation 12:17; 14:12). He also alluded to specific commandments of the Decalogue, such as the second (1 John 5:21), sixth (1 John 3:12), and the ninth (1 John 2:4). Again it is noteworthy that, although the word *Sabbath* does not occur in his epistles, John stresses the perpetuity of the Decalogue, which includes the Sabbath.

The book of Jude

In verse 5 of his book, Jude recalls the timing of the Exodus during which time God spoke the Decalogue on Mount Sinai: "I want to remind you, though you once knew this, that the Lord, having saved the people out of the land of Egypt, afterward destroyed those who did not believe." Jude also describes the sexual immorality of Sodom and Gomorrah in verse 7. Whenever a judgment is administered, laws have been broken.

Note the connection between judgment and ungodly deeds in Jude's account of Enoch. "Now Enoch, the seventh from Adam, prophesied about these men also, saying, 'Behold, the Lord comes with ten thousands of His saints, to execute judgment on all, to convict all who are ungodly among them of all their ungodly deeds which they have committed in an ungodly way, and of all the harsh things which ungodly sinners have spoken against Him' " (Jude 14, 15).

Summary of the general epistles

Though the word *Sabbath* does not appear in the general epistles, but it is clearly included in the references to the law and the commandments. There is no evidence that the law had been or would be changed or canceled or that the seventh-day Sabbath was being replaced by another day. Instead, there is an unmistakable continuation of the Old Testament Decalogue in the epistles. Law-keeping is emphatically urged.

The book of Revelation

The full title of the last book in the New Testament and, of course, in the Bible, is "The Revelation of Jesus Christ." In the opening chapter, John the revelator mentions that he was "on the island that is called Patmos" and that he "was in the Spirit on the Lord's Day" (Revelation 1:9, 10). The phrase "the Lord's Day" still generates divergence of interpretation. The difficulty lies in the fact that the phrase is a hapax legomenon, meaning that this exact phrase cannot be found anywhere else in the New Testament.

Many commentators, ancient and modern, have decided that "the Lord's day" (*kuriake hemera*) refers to Sunday, the first day of the week. Undergirding this thinking are the interpretations of second-century writers, especially in two early second-century writings: the *Didache* and the letter of Ignatius of Antioch to the Magnesians. They interpreted "the Lord's day" this way because Jesus rose from the dead on Sunday. However, these documents were written nearly a whole century after the book of Revelation was written, meaning they were written too late to be helpful in interpretation.

The record of the rise of Sunday sacredness is very complex, with the change to Sunday sacredness being very gradual. In Eastern Christianity, it involved the keeping of both days for several centuries. It was not until the fourth century that Sunday keeping eclipsed the biblical Sabbath—which will be reviewed in the next chapter.

Another interpretation for "the Lord's Day" contends that it refers to Easter Sunday—celebrated annually rather than weekly. But this position is not strongly supported historically, though different Christian groups have celebrated Easter Sunday for centuries.

Seventh-day Adventists believe that "the Lord's Day" means the seventh-day Sabbath, and support this position intertextually:

- In Isaiah 58:13, Deity refers to the Sabbath as His—"*My holy day*"—and urges us to "call the Sabbath a delight, *the holy day of the* LORD honorable" (emphasis added).
- All three synoptic gospels quote Jesus saying: "The Son of Man is also Lord of the Sabbath" (Matthew 12:8; Mark 2:28; Luke 6:5).
- Christians of the first century would rightly have understood John as describing his vision on the seventh-day Sabbath because there is no indication of a change of day in the New Testament.
- Historically, a second-century document, *The Martyrdom of Polycarp*, describes the punishing death of Polycarp, bishop of Smyrna—mentioning that he was captured on "the day of the preparation," or Friday, and that his martyrdom took place on "the great Sabbath."[6] These two expressions of two different days demonstrate that Christians in Smyrna around the middle of the second century were still thinking of Friday as "the preparation day" before the Sabbath—just as Luke does in his gospel (as discussed earlier, Luke 23:54).

The three angels' messages of Revelation 14:6–12 point to a climactic worldwide pronouncement of the "everlasting gospel" with "the hour of His [God's] judgment." The gospel is presented as "everlasting"! It is the only time in Scripture that these two terms are used together. The word *everlasting* is used many times, as is the word *gospel*. But only here in the first angel's message are they used together. This phrase means that the gospel has never changed! That the angel announcement is given with a "loud voice" underscores its decisive importance.

Additionally, there are strong parallels of wording between Exodus 20:11 and Revelation 14:7, which indicate that the message of the first angel of Revelation 14 has something to do with the Sabbath—and that the Sabbath has to do with worship. We were not made for ourselves, but for fellowship with our Creator. In fact, the Sabbath is one of the great proofs that God is love—for lovers like to set apart specific times to be together.

What is more, divine judgment being linked with the everlasting gospel is of enormous importance. For one thing, there can be no judgment—nor could there even need to be a judgment—without law. This judgment in Revelation 14 is a divine judgment, which connects it to God's law—that law, of course, including the fourth commandment about the Sabbath. Moreover, being linked with the "everlasting gospel" makes the law (including the Sabbath) and final judgment good news!

The fourth commandment itself marks the link between the Creation of the world and the Sabbath, as we reviewed earlier. The first angel's message, uniting divine judgment with the everlasting gospel, suggests that the two have been wrongly separated and need to be united again. Yes, divine judgment is good news!

The second angel's message deals with Babylon's "fornication," which likewise implies an ethical issue, also entailing a standard of law.

The third angel's message further clarifies this, underscoring that true and/or false worship is involved. In verse 12, the "patience of the saints" is given identifying markers. The "saints" will

- "keep the commandments of God"—keeping God's commandments also refers to the Decalogue, which of course, would include the Sabbath commandment—and

- have the "faith of Jesus"—which again connects the everlasting gospel (verse 6)!

This is a double restoration of both the law and the gospel. They are often thought to be in contradiction with each other, but they belong together! Seventh-day Adventists are not legalists. Nor are we just speaking sweetly of Jesus and His love. Instead, we teach and follow the angels' messages of Revelation 14, upholding the biblical connection of faith and works.

The Sabbath links Creation and Redemption because the Creator and Redeemer are the same Person! Paul is one of many Bible writers who stresses Jesus as Creator. For example, he expresses his prayer for the Colossians, that they would be

giving thanks to the Father who has qualified us to be partakers of the inheritance of the saints in the light. He has delivered us from the power of darkness and conveyed us into the kingdom of the Son of His love, in whom we have redemption through His blood, the forgiveness of sins.

He is the image of the invisible God, the firstborn over all creation. For by Him all things were created that are in heaven and that are on earth, visible and invisible, whether thrones or dominions or principalities or powers. All things were created through Him and for Him. And He is before all things, and in Him all things consist. And He is the head of the body, the church, who is the beginning, the firstborn from the dead, that in all things He may have the preeminence (Colossians 1:12–18).

The heavenly angel chorus also chants praises to the Lamb, Jesus the Redeemer, in one of the two worship scenes described in Revelation:

Now when He had taken the scroll, the four living creatures and the twenty-four elders fell down before the Lamb, each having a harp, and golden bowls full of incense, which are the prayers of the saints. And they sang a new song, saying:

> "You are worthy to take the scroll,
> And to open its seals;
> For You were slain,
> And have redeemed us to God by Your blood
> Out of every tribe and tongue and people and nation,
> And have made us kings and priests to our God;
> And we shall reign on the earth" (Revelation 5:8–10).

Yes, the Lord Jesus is the Creator and Redeemer—and He calls Himself "Lord of the Sabbath" and, in Matthew 11:28, the giver of true rest. As we noted earlier, immediately after Jesus declared His promised rest, it was linked with a Sabbath incident that illuminates it. Jesus both created the Sabbath and offers salvation. He didn't ignore, eliminate, or change the Sabbath when He died on the cross. Through the prophet Isaiah, He promised it would continue forever! Jesus even exalted the Sabbath as a Sabbath keeper: "as His custom was" is how Luke describes it. His disciples were Sabbath keepers, too, as we saw above.

Nevertheless, for some, it is difficult to understand the relationship between the Sabbath and salvation. Is it only a matter of which day? Is it a matter of needing to keep it to be saved? Or are both a matter of a genuine relationship with Jesus, the Creator? These are crucial issues that need to be understood.

As reviewed earlier, Adam and Eve were given the Sabbath before they sinned and before they had even worked—so they couldn't have been keeping the Sabbath to be saved from sin—nor working to earn salvation. Their very first full day was the Sabbath. "And on the seventh day God ended His work which He had done, and He rested on the seventh day from all His work which He had done. Then God blessed the seventh day and sanctified it, because in it He rested from all His work which God had created and made" (Genesis 2:2, 3).

Instead of keeping the Sabbath to be saved, it is a gift—like salvation itself! The blessed seventh day is a gift of divine grace. Sabbath rest is not produced by humans, nor can it be earned by human effort. It is not something we create or achieve. Nor is it a reward. Instead, it comes to us as a gift from the Creator, who demonstrates that He is sovereign even over time!

Notably, the doctrine of the divine creation of space and time is linked and intertwined with many other biblical doctrines:

- tithing: returning to God a small portion of what He created
- Christ's incarnation: Jesus assumed the human flesh He created
- Christ's atonement: The Savior died to save the humans He created
- Christ's second coming: He returns to reclaim what He made
- the Sabbath: a weekly memorial and celebration of this divinely created, blessed, and soon-to-be-saved world

The blessed parameters of the Sabbath are vast and all-encompassing! It is truly amazing that there has been confusion about which day. The source of this confusion will be seen as we leave the New Testament and turn to a brief historical survey of what happened to the seventh-day Sabbath.

---

1. Ellen G. White, *Steps to Christ* (Washington, DC: Review and Herald®, 1956), 11, 12.

2. Ellen G. White, *The Desire of Ages* (Mountain View, CA: Pacific Press®, 1940), 207.

3. White, 286, 287.

4. Ellen G. White, *Selected Messages*, book 1 (Washington, DC: Review and Herald®, 1958), 344.

5. See, for example, Ralph P. Martin, *James*, Word Biblical Commentary, vol. 48 (Waco, TX: Word, 1988); Virgil V. Orter Jr., "The Sermon on the Mount in the Book of James, Part 1," *Bibliotheca Sacra* 162 (July–September 2005): 344–360; Virgil V. Porter Jr., "The Sermon on the Mount in the Book of James, Part 2," *Bibliotheca Sacra* 162 (October–December 2005): 470–482.

6. *The Martyrdom of Polycarp*, 7.1; 8:1; 21.1, in *The Ante-Nicene Fathers*, ed. Alexander Roberts and James Donaldson, 1885–1887, vol. 1 (Peabody, MA: Hendrickson, 1994), 40, 43.

Chapter Five

After the New Testament:
What Happened?

The growth and spread of the first-century Christian Church documented in the New Testament book of Acts was vigorous—with Christians and new Gentile converts worshiping together each Sabbath, as we saw in the last chapter. The church continued to grow, and interest in the Sabbath by the church fathers and other writers persisted. The day obviously continued to be held in high esteem. Though existing records from the first centuries are not copious, there are Sabbath sentiments to be found. In this chapter, we will peruse a brief sprinkling of evidence for the continuance of the Sabbath within many different cultures for the next twenty centuries.

The first century
Hadrian (76–138). It seems that in Rome and Alexandria, anti-Jewish laws, including laws against keeping the Sabbath, were enacted by Emperor Hadrian because of strong anti-Jewish sentiments at that time. His laws apparently were not evenly enforced throughout the empire, however.

Hadrian's laws outlawing Sabbath observance primarily targeted the Jews because of the bloody Jewish revolts the Romans had had to deal with. Finally, they completely destroyed the Jerusalem temple and built Roman temples on the site. Jews were barred from entering Jerusalem—though Christians could.

Sabbath-keeping Christians worked within the anti-Sabbath laws by doing good deeds on the seventh day—taking their cue from Jesus' Sabbath activities.

Philo of Alexandria (20 BC–AD 50). Philo was a Jewish contemporary of Jesus but born and raised in Alexandria, Egypt. He wrote that the seventh day was the completion of Creation, "for it is the festival, not of a single city or country, but of the universe, and it alone strictly deserves to be called 'public' as belonging to all people and the birthday of the world."[1] He also wrote that the Sabbath was not only for the Jews. "Every seventh day is sacred, which is called by the Hebrews the sabbath; and the seventh month in every year has the greatest of the festivals allotted to it, so that very naturally the seventh year also has a share of the veneration paid to this number, and receives especial honour."[2]

The fourth commandment has reference to the sacred seventh day, that it may be passed in a sacred and holy manner. Now some states keep the holy festival only once in the month, counting from the new moon, as a day sacred to God; but the nation of the Jews keep every seventh day regularly, after each interval of six days; and there is an account of events recorded in the history of the creation of the world, comprising a sufficient relation of the cause of this ordinance; for the sacred historian says, that the world was created in six days, and that on the seventh day God desisted from his works, and began to contemplate what he had so beautifully created; therefore, he commanded the beings also who were destined to live in this state, to imitate God in this particular also, as well as in all others, applying themselves to their works for six days, but desisting from them and philosophising on the seventh day, and devoting their leisure to the contemplation of the things of nature, and considering whether in the preceding six days they have done anything which has not been holy, bringing their conduct before the judgment-seat of the soul, and subjecting it to a scrutiny, and making themselves give an account of all the things which they have said or done; the laws sitting by as assessors and joint inquirers, in order to the correcting of such errors as have been committed through carelessness, and to the guarding against any similar offences being hereafter repeated.[3]

"The fourth commandment," Philo says, "deals with the sacred seventh day, that it should be observed in a reverent and religious manner. . . . [Men should] rest on the seventh and turn to the study of wisdom."[4]

Philo concludes: "Again, the experience of those who keep the seventh day is that both body and soul are benefited in two most essential ways. The body is benefited by the recurrence of respite from continuous and wearisome toil, the soul by the excellent conceptions which it receives of God as the worldmaker and guardian of what He has begotten. For He brought all things to their completion on the seventh day. These things shew clearly that he who gives due value to the seventh day gains value for himself."[5]

"On this day we are commanded to abstain from all work, not because the law inculcates slackness; on the contrary it always inures men to endure hardship and incites them to labour. . . . Its object is rather to give men relaxation from continuous and unending toil and by refreshing their bodies with a regularly calculated system of remissions, to send them out renewed to their old activities. . . . Further, when He [God] forbids bodily labour on the seventh day, He permits the exercise of the higher activities, namely, those employed in the study of the principles of virtue's lore."[6]

The second to the third century
Tertullian (160–220). Tertullian was a lawyer who had carefully

penned arguments. He wrote that it is lawful to do good on the Sabbath: "For when it says of the Sabbath-day, 'In it thou shalt not do any work of thine,' by the word *thine* it restricts prohibition to human work—which every one performs in his own employment or business—and not to divine work."[7]

Tertullian also addressed "Christ's defense of His disciples when they picked and ate grain on the Sabbath:

". . . But because He did not directly defend His disciples, but excuses them; because He interposes human want, as if deprecating censure; because He maintains the honour of the Sabbath as a day which is to be free from gloom rather than from work; because he puts David and his companions on a level with His own disciples in their fault and their extenuation; because He is pleased to endorse the Creator's indulgence; because He is Himself good according to His example—is He therefore alien from the Creator?

". . . Christ maintained the honor of the Sabbath as a day to be 'free from gloom rather than from work.' "[8]

Tertullian also defined his understanding of "work." Repeating his earlier statements, he expands his explanation:

The Pharisees, however, were in utter error concerning the law of the Sabbath, not observing that its terms were conditional, when it enjoined rest from labour, making certain distinctions of labour. For when it says of the Sabbath-day, "In it thou shalt not do any work of thine," by the word *thine* it restricts the prohibition to human work—which every one performs in his own employment or business—and not to divine work. Now the work of healing or preserving is not proper to man, but to God. . . .Wishing, therefore, to initiate them into this meaning of the law by the restoration of the withered hand, He inquires, "Is it lawful on the Sabbath-days to do good, or not? to save life, or to destroy it?" In order that He might, whilst allowing that amount of work which He was about to perform for a soul, remind them what works the law of the Sabbath forbade—even human works; and what it enjoined—even divine works, which might be done for the benefit of any soul, He was called "Lord of the Sabbath," because He maintained the Sabbath as His own institution.[9]

Again, he maintained that the Sabbath was not lost "at the destruction of Jericho" and then goes on to say:

"Now, although He has in a certain place expressed an aversion of Sabbaths, by calling them *your Sabbaths*, reckoning them as men's Sabbaths, not His own, because they were celebrated without the fear of God by a people full of iniquities, and loving God "with the lip, not the heart," He has yet put His own Sabbaths (those, that is, which were kept according to His prescription) in a different position; for by the same prophet, in a later passage, He declared them to be "true, and delightful, and inviolable." Thus Christ did not at all rescind the Sabbath: He kept the law thereof. . . . He exhibits in a clear light the different kinds of work, while doing what the law excepts from the sacredness of the Sabbath *and* while imparting to the Sabbath-day itself, which from the beginning had been consecrated by the benediction of the Father, an additional sanctity by His own beneficent action. For He furnished to this day divine safeguards. . . . Since, in like manner, the prophet Elisha on this day restored to life the dead son of the Shunammite woman, you see, O Pharisee, and you too, O Marcion, how that it was *proper employment* for the Creator's Sabbaths of old to do good, to save life, not to destroy it; how that Christ introduced nothing new, which was not after the example, the gentleness, the mercy, and the prediction also of the Creator.[10]

Another reference to the Sabbath can be found in book 4, discussing the matter about healing on the Sabbath:

When the question was again raised concerning a cure performed on the Sabbath-day, how did He discuss it: "Doth not each of you on the Sabbath loose his ass or his ox from the stall, and lead him away to watering?" When, therefore, He did a work according to the condition prescribed by the law, He affirmed, instead of breaking, the law, which commanded that no work should be done, except what might be done for any living being; *and if for any one*, then how much more for a *human* life?[11]

Origen (185–254). "After the festival of the unceasing sacrifice [the Crucifixion] is put the second festival of the Sabbath, and it is fitting for whoever is righteous among the saints to keep also the festival of the Sabbath. Which is, indeed, the festival of the Sabbath, except that concerning which the Apostle said, 'There remaineth therefore a sabbatismus, that is, a keeping of the Sabbath, to the people of God [Hebrews 4:9]'? Forsaking therefore the Judaic observance of the Sabbath, let us see what sort of observance of the Sabbath is expected of the Christian. On the day of the Sabbath nothing of worldly acts ought to be performed." [12]

Irenaeus (130–202). Irenaeus wrote that Christ did not do away with the Decalogue or even the Sabbath commandment: "Perfect righteousness was conferred neither by any other legal ceremonies. The Decalogue however was not canceled by Christ, but is always in force: men were never released from its commandments."[13]

Justin Martyr (100–165). Justin did some allegorizing of the meaning of the Sabbath as had the gnostics—who were influencing those in Rome and Alexandria by this time: "If there is any perjured person or a thief among you, let him cease to be so; if any adulterer, let him repent; then he has kept the sweet and true sabbaths of God."[14]

Theophilus, Bishop of Antioch (169–182). Theophilus wrote: "And on the sixth day God finished His works which He made, and rested on the seventh day from all His works which He made. And God blessed the seventh day, and sanctified it; because in it He rested from all His works which God began to create."[15]

"Moreover, [they spoke] concerning the seventh day, which all men acknowledge; but the most know not that what among the Hebrews is called the 'Sabbath,' is translated into Greek the 'Seventh' (ἑβδομάς), a name which is adopted by every nation, although they know not the reason of the appellation."[16]

Other attitudes about the Sabbath continued, with the Roman emperor Constantine weighing in. Even so, Sabbath keeping spread west into Europe, east into India, and even into China.

The third century

"As early as A.D. 225 there existed large bishoprics or conferences of the Church of the East stretching from Palestine to, and surrounding, India" that were Sabbath keeping.[17]

The Kushan Dynasty of North India called a famous council of Buddhist priests at Vaiśāli "to bring uniformity among the Buddhist monks on the observance of their weekly Sabbath. They had been so impressed by the Old Testament writings that they had begun to keep the seventh-day."[18]

From surviving records, it appears that various imperial edicts and ecclesiastical ordinances caused Sunday sacredness to slowly rise to a position of honor within Christianity. The first public measure legalizing Sunday observance was Constantine's law in 321, which required people in the city to rest on the venerable day of the sun but permitted those living in the countryside to continue their agricultural tasks. Two years later, Constantine assumed the Christian religion and, thereafter, enforced his law.

Though a Roman mandate, many Christians did not accept the Sunday substitute as having divine authority. However, the bishop of Rome soon conferred the title of "Lord's Day" on the first day of the week. Another bishop, who was a friend and flatterer of Emperor Constantine, claimed that Christ had transferred the Sabbath to Sunday—but without any proof from Scripture.

The fourth century

Athanasius (296–373). Athanasius of Alexandria wrote about Christians holding "religious assemblies on the sabbath, not because they were infected with Judaism, but to worship Jesus the Lord of the Sabbath. Epiphanius says the same."[19]

Ambrose (339–397). Ambrose of Milan stated that the Abyssinian bishop Museus had "traveled almost everywhere in the country of the Seres [China]." Ambrose also mentioned that when he was in Milan, he observed Saturday, but when in Rome observed Sunday, giving rise to the proverb: "When you are in Rome, do as Rome does."[20]

Both Saturday and Sunday were revered in different places. The Abyssinian Church, however, continued to sanctify Saturday as the holy day for centuries.[21]

"Ambrose sanctified the seventh day as the Sabbath (as he himself says). Ambrose had great influence in Spain, which was also observing the Saturday Sabbath."[22]

The Council of Laodicea (365). The Sabbath was on the agenda at the church council held in Laodicea and is mentioned in its edicts.

(1) Canon 16: "On Saturday the Gospels and other portions of the Scripture shall be read aloud."

(2) Canon 29: "Christians shall not Judaize and be idle on Saturday, but shall work on that day; but the Lord's day they shall

especially honour, as being Christians, shall, if possible, do no work on that day."[23]

The fifth century

Augustine (354–430). Augustine of Hippo deplored the fact that in two neighboring churches in Africa, one observed the seventh-day Sabbath while another fasted on it.[24]

Sidonius (430–489). Sidonius explained (speaking of King Theodoric of the Goths, 454–526), "It is a fact that it was formerly the custom in the East to keep the Sabbath in the same manner as the Lord's day and to hold sacred assemblies: while on the other hand, the people of the West, contending for the Lord's day have neglected the celebration of the Sabbath."[25]

Sozomen (400–450). According to the church historian Sozomen, "The people of Constantinople and almost everywhere, assemble together on the Sabbath, as well as on the first day of the week, which custom is never observed at Rome or at Alexandria."[26] Speaking of what is now called the Middle East, he said, "There are several cities and villages in Egypt where, contrary to the usage established elsewhere, the people meet together on Sabbath evenings, and, although they have dined previously, partake of the mysteries."[27]

The sixth and seventh centuries

The bishops of Rome continued to assume headship over the church, and during this period, the exaltation of Sunday advanced.

> For a time the people engaged in agricultural labor when not attending church, and the name Sabbath was still attached to the seventh day. But steadily and surely a change was effected. Those in holy office were forbidden to pass judgment in any civil controversy on the Sunday. Soon after, persons of all rank were commanded to refrain from common labor, on pain of

a fine for freemen, and stripes in the case of servants. Later it was decreed that rich men should be punished with the loss of half of their estates; and finally, that if still obstinate they should be made slaves. The lower classes were to suffer perpetual banishment.[28]

Miracles were reported, supposedly substantiating Sunday sacredness.

It was reported that as a husbandman who was about to plow his field on Sunday, cleaned his plow with an iron, the iron stuck fast in his hand, and for two years he carried it about with him, "to his exceeding great pain and shame."

Later, the pope gave directions that the parish priest should admonish the violators of Sunday, and wish them to go to church and say their prayers, lest they bring some great calamity on themselves and neighbors. An ecclesiastical council brought forward the argument since so widely employed, that because persons had been struck by lightning while laboring on Sunday, it must be the Sabbath. "It is apparent," said the prelates, "how high the displeasure of God was upon their neglect of this day." An appeal was then made that priests and ministers, kings and princes, and all faithful people, "use their utmost endeavors and care that the day be restored to its honor, and, for the credit of Christianity, more devoutly observed for time to come."

The decrees of councils proving insufficient, the secular authorities were besought to issue an edict that would strike terror to the hearts of the people, and force them to refrain from labor on the Sunday. At a synod held in Rome, all previous decisions were reaffirmed with greater force and solemnity. They were also incorporated into the ecclesiastical law, and enforced by the civil authorities throughout nearly all Christendom.

After the New Testament: What Happened?

Still the absence of scriptural authority for Sunday-keeping occasioned no little embarrassment. The people questioned the right of their teachers to deny the positive declaration of Jehovah, "The seventh day is the Sabbath of the Lord thy God," in order to honor the day of the sun.[29]

In Ireland. "We seem to see here an allusion to the custom, observed in the early monastic church of Ireland, of keeping the day of rest on Saturday, or the Sabbath."[30]

In Scotland. " 'Having continued his [Columba's] labours in Scotland thirty-four years, he clearly and openly foretold his death, and on Saturday, the month of June, said to his disciple Diermit: "This day is called the Sabbath, that is the rest day, and such will it truly be to me; for it will put an end to my labours." ' *Butler's Lives of the Saints*, Vol. 1, A.D. 597, art. 'St. Columba' p. 762."[31]

" 'It seems to have been customary in the Celtic churches of early times, in Ireland as well as Scotland, to keep Saturday, the Jewish Sabbath, as a day of rest from labour. They obeyed the fourth commandment literally upon the seventh day of the week.' James C. Moffatt, D.D., Professor of Church History at Princeton *The Church in Scotland*, p. 140."[32]

" 'The Celts used a Latin Bible unlike the Vulgate (R.C.) and kept Saturday as a day of rest, with special religious services on Sunday.' Flick, *The Rise of Mediaeval Church*, p. 237."[33]

The eighth century

Italy. The Council of Friaul, 791 (Canon 13): "We command all Christians to observe the Lord's day to be held not in honor of the past Sabbath, but on account of that holy night of the first of the week called the Lord's day. When speaking of that Sabbath which the Jews observe, the last day of the week, and which also our peasants observe."[34]

In Persia and Mesopotamia. "The hills of Persia and the valleys of the Tigris and Euphrates reechoed their songs of praise. They reaped their harvests and paid their tithes. They repaired to their churches on the Sabbath day for the worship of God."[35]

In India, China, and Persia. "Widespread and enduring was the observance of the seventh-day Sabbath among the believers of the Church of the East and the St. Thomas Christians of India, who never were connected with Rome. It also was maintained among those bodies which broke off from Rome after the Council of Chalcedon namely, the Abyssinians, the Jacobites, the Maronites, and the Armenians."[36]

In AD 781 the famous China Monument was inscribed in marble to tell of the growth of Christianity in China at that time. The inscription, consisting of 763 words, was unearthed in 1625 near the city of Changan and now stands in the "Forest of Tablets," Changan. The following extract from the stone shows that Sabbath was observed: "On the seventh day we offer sacrifices, after having purified our hearts, and received absolution for our sins. This religion, so perfect and so excellent, is difficult to name, but it enlightens darkness by its brilliant precepts."[37]

The ninth and tenth centuries

In Bulgaria. " 'Bulgaria, in the early season of its evangelization had been taught that no work should be performed on the Sabbath.' *Responsa Nicolai Papae I* and *Con-Consulta Bullillgarorum, Responsum 10, found in Mansi, Sacrorum Concilorum Nova et Amplissima Colectio,* Vol. 15, p. 406; also Hefele, *Conciliengeschicte,* Vol. 4, sec. 478."[38]

In Scotland. " 'They worked on Sunday, but kept Saturday in a Sabbatical manner.' Andrew Lang, *A History of Scotland from the Roman Occupation,* Vol. I, p. 96."[39]

In the Church of the East/Kurdistan. " 'The Nestorians eat no pork and keep the Sabbath. They believe in neither auricular confession nor purgatory.' Schaff-Herzog, *The New Encyclopaedia of Religious Knowledge*, art. 'Nestorians.' "[40]

The eleventh to fourteenth centuries

In Ireland and Scotland. " 'They held that Saturday was properly the Sabbath on which they abstained from work.' Skene, *Celtic Scotland*, Vol. 2, p. 350."[41]

" 'T. Ratcliffe Barnett, in his book on the fervent Catholic queen of Scotland who in 1060 was first to attempt to ruin Columba's brethren, writes: "In this matter the Scots had perhaps kept up the traditional usage of the ancient Irish Church which observed Saturday instead of Sunday as the day of rest." ' Barnett, *Margaret of Scotland: Queen and Saint*, p. 97."[42]

In Constantinople. " 'Because you [Christians] observe the Sabbath with the Jews and the Lord's Day with us, you seem to imitate with such observance the sect of Nazarenes.' Migne, *Patrologia Latina*, Vol. 145, p. 506; see also Hergenroether, *Photius*, Vol. 3, p. 746."[43]

In Lombardy. "Traces of Sabbath-keepers are found in the times of Gregory I, Gregory VII, and in the twelfth century in Lombardy."[44]

The Waldenses. "Some of the Waldenses of the Alps . . . were called *Sabbati, Sabbatati, Insabbatati*, but more frequently *Inzabbatati*. One says they were so named from the Hebrew word Sabbath, because they kept the Saturday for the Lord's day."[45]

"Among the documents [of the Waldenses], an explanation of the Ten Commandments [was] dated by Boyer to 1120. Observance of the Sabbath by ceasing from worldly labours, is enjoined."[46] Moreover, fourteenth-century portrayals quote the Waldenses: " 'That we are to worship one only God, who is able to help us, and not the Saints departed; that we ought to keep holy the Sabbath day.' Luther, *Fore-runners*, p. 38."[47]

The sixteenth century

Martin Luther. Luther's earliest comments on the Sabbath appear in his *First Lectures on Psalms*, written from 1513 to 1515 when he was a young teacher at Wittenberg. He was still influenced by his Catholic background and thought that *Sabbath* referred to Sunday. Nevertheless, he sought to encourage believers with a deeper Sabbath experience, explaining that the reason for keeping the Sabbath was because the Creator rested and sanctified the Sabbath day. In fact, he taught that God's sanctification of the Sabbath was important and He considers His works "so great that He commands us not only to keep the day of rest, but also to hallow it or regard it as holy."[48]

In his sermon "The Gospel for the Festival of the Epiphany," Luther clearly taught that it is God's works that sanctify the Sabbath, not ours: "For what you do is not of yourself, but entirely God's work within you."[49]

Luther connected the Sabbath to Creation, especially in his *Lectures on Genesis* (beginning in 1535 and continuing nearly ten years). He mentioned the special purpose for the Sabbath was in "making us understand that the seventh day in particular should be devoted to divine worship. For 'holy' is that which has been set aside for God and has been removed from all secular uses. Hence to sanctify means to set aside for sacred purposes, or for the worship of God."[50] Also, "man was especially created for the knowledge and worship of God. . . . On the seventh day He wanted men to busy themselves both with His Word and with the other forms of worship established by Him, so that we might give first thought to the fact that this nature was created chiefly for acknowledging and glorifying God."[51]

Luther believed that Adam kept the seventh day sacred and would have continued keeping it if he had not sinned: "On this day [Adam] would have given his descendants instructions about the will and worship of God; he would have praised God; he would have given thanks; he should have sacrificed, etc. On the other days he would have tilled his fields and tended his cattle."[52]

He wrote that the Old Testament patriarchs were obedient to the Decalogue and that there would be a Sabbath during the coming millennium. But because of his Catholic background, he believed that Christ abolished the Jewish Sabbath as a literal day of rest on the seventh day of the week and that the Sabbath was ceremonial and a shadow. Nevertheless, he affirmed Sabbath keeping: "But whoever wants to make a necessary command of the Sabbath as a work required of God, must keep Saturday, and not Sunday; for Saturday was enjoined upon the Jews, and not Sunday. But Christians have thus far kept Sunday, and not Saturday, because Christ arose on that day. This is a certain sign that the Sabbath, and the whole of Moses, do not concern us in the least; otherwise we ought to keep Saturday."[53]

Luther commented on the Sabbath many times, acknowledging its importance. Though not consistent in upholding the seventh day, he does continue in the strong Christian tradition of maintaining the importance of the Sabbath.

John Calvin. Calvin's understanding and views are very similar to Luther's. He, too, focused on God's resting, blessing, and sanctifying the Sabbath at Creation. His extensive writings include a number of commentaries, among which is one on Genesis. In it, he connects the Sabbath with God completing His work of creating: "God ceased from all his work, when he desisted from the creation of new kinds of things. . . . This language is intended merely to express the perfection of the fabric of the world."[54] Calvin also explained the Sabbath rest God intended for humanity: "God did not command men simply to keep holiday every seventh day, as if he delighted in their indolence; but rather that they, being released from all other business, might more readily apply their minds to the Creator of the world."[55]

He held that the Sabbath commandment in the Decalogue still

continues because the three causes were not abolished. It remains relevant for Christians who need spiritual rest in worship and a time of rest for servants, "for we know how prone men are to fall into indifference, unless they have some props to lean on or some stimulants to arouse them in maintaining their care and zeal for religion."[56] In concert with medieval Christianity, Calvin continued to defend the change of Sabbath to Sunday. Nevertheless, he also continued the long Christian tradition of defending the importance of Sabbath.

In England. In 1657, the British Parliament, in response to mounting pressure from Sabbath-keeping leaders in London and their publications, appointed a committee to investigate the observance of the seventh-day Sabbath. There is no record whether any committee reported results or whether any report was made public. Three years later, the former Puritan clergyman Theophilus Brabourne claimed that the Sabbath question was "the highest controversy in the Church of England" at the time.[57] And in 1671, the influential Independent minister Dr. John Owen expressed the fear that "many might yet turn to the seventh day."[58]

During this time, the Puritans called for a purer church in England, cleansed from medieval Catholic elements. The Bible for the Puritans was the divinely inspired Word of God that contained standards of belief and worship. The "Sabbatarian Controversy" began in 1595 with the publication of Nicholas Bownd's book *The Doctrine of the Sabbath*. With this book, the Puritans began calling for a more biblical observation of Sunday than what currently prevailed in the Church of England.

Bownd's book contained several arguments still valid in defense of the Sabbath: (1) the Sabbath was instituted at Creation and originated with Adam and not the Jews; (2) the fourth commandment of the Decalogue was as moral as the other nine, and thereby perpetually binding rather than ceremonial for it predated all Jewish ceremonies; (3) Christians, as were the Jews, are obligated to keep the original seventh day; (4) in all the other nine commandments God forbids the sin and assumes the virtue, but in the fourth commandment He both commands the good and forbids the evil.

Even so, the Puritans believed the Sabbath had been transferred from the seventh day to the first day in honor of Christ's resurrection. The change was defended on the grounds that the Sabbath commandment called for one day of rest after six days of labor. The actual day of rest could thus be changed without losing the inherently moral nature of the commandment. Apostolic authority was claimed to be behind the change.

The seventeenth and eighteenth centuries

In England. The Seventh Day Baptists became a leading Sabbatarian church. Their first church in America was founded in Newport, Rhode Island, in 1671.*

"Here are, in England [1668], about nine or ten churches that keep the Sabbath, besides many scattered disciples, who have been eminently preserved in this tottering day."[59] Notable also is the inscription on the monument over the grave of Dr. Peter Chamberlen, physician to King James and Queen Anne, King Charles I, and Queen Katherine. It states that Dr. Chamberlen was "a Christian keeping ye Commandments of God & [the] faith of Jesus, being baptized about ye year 1648, & keeping ye 7th day for ye Saboth about 32 years."[60]

Voltaire (1694–1778)—no friend of the church—declared: "If you wish to destroy the Christian religion you must first destroy the Christian Sunday."[61]

In Sweden and Finland. " 'We can trace these opinions over

---

* Seventh-day Adventists acknowledge that their understanding of the biblical Sabbath is indebted to the Seventh Day Baptists. This is reflected in the first volume of the *Advent Review and the Sabbath Herald*, for over half the material was reprinted from Seventh Day Baptist publications. See Raymond F. Cottrell, "Seventh Day Baptists and Adventists: A Common Heritage," *Spectrum* 9 (1977): 3–8.

almost the whole extent of Sweden of that day—from Finland and northern Sweden.' 'In the district of Upsala the farmers kept Saturday in place of Sunday. About the year 1625 this religious tendency became so pronounced in these countries that not only large numbers of the common people began to keep Saturday as the rest day, but even many priests did the same.' *History of the Swedish Church*, Vol. I, p. 256."[62]

In Russia. It was said of the Russian Muscovite Church: " 'They solemnize Saturday (the old Sabbath).' Samuel Purchase, *His Pilgrims*. Vol. I, p. 350."[63]

In India. The Jacobites, in 1625, " 'kept Saturday holy. They have solemn service on Saturdays.' Pilgrimmes, Part 2, p. 1269."[64]

In America. " 'Stephen Mumford, the first Sabbath-keeper in America, came from London in 1664.' *History of the Seventh-day Baptist General Conference* by Jas. Bailey, pp. 237, 238."[65]

Count Zinzendorf, in 1738, "wrote of his keeping the Sabbath . . . : 'That I have employed the Sabbath for rest many years already, and our Sunday for the proclamation of the gospel.' *Budingsche Sammlung*, Sec. 8, p. 224. Leipzig, 1742."[66] After Zinzendorf arrived from Europe, it is recorded of the Moravian Brethren: " 'As a special instance it deserves to be noticed that he is resolved with the church at Bethlehem to observe the seventh day as rest day.' Ibid., pp. 5, 1421, 1422."[67] Yet, "before Zinzendorf and the Moravians at Bethlehem [observed] the Sabbath and prospered, there [already] was a small body of German Sabbath-keepers in Pennsylvania. See Rupp's *History of Religious Denominations in the United States*, pp. 109–123."[68]

In Germany. " 'He [Tennhardt of Nuremberg] holds strictly to the doctrine of the Sabbath, because it is one of the ten commandments.' Bengel's *Leban und Wirken*, Burk, p. 579."[69]

In Abyssinia. " 'The Jacobites assembled on the Sabbath day, before the Domical day, in the temple, and kept that day, as do also the Abyssinians as we have seen from the confession of their faith by the Ethiopian king Claudius.' Abundacnus, *Historia Jaco-batarum*, p. 118–9."[70]

The nineteenth and twentieth centuries

In China. " 'At this time Hung prohibited the use of opium, and even tobacco, and all intoxicating drinks, and the Sabbath was religiously observed.' *The Ti-Ping Revolution*, by Llin-Le, an officer among them, Vol. 1, pp. 36–48, 84."[71] Also: The seventh day is most religiously and strictly observed. "The Taiping Sabbath is kept upon our Saturday. . . . The Taipings when asked why they observed the seventh day Sabbath, replied that it was, first, because the Bible taught it, and second, because their ancestors observed it as a day of worship."[72]

In India and Persia. "Besides, they maintain the solemn observance of Christian worship throughout our empire on the seventh day."[73]

In Sweden. Baptists: "We will now endeavor to show that the sanctification of the Sabbath has its foundation and its origin in a law which God at creation itself established for the whole world, and as a consequence thereof is binding on all men in all ages."[74]

In America. The Seventh-day Adventist Church grew out of the Great Disappointment in 1844. Ellen White, one of the pioneers, wrote eloquently about the true biblical Sabbath.

> The great Jehovah had laid the foundations of the earth; He had dressed the whole world in the garb of beauty and had filled it with things useful to man; He had created all the wonders of the land and of the sea. In six days the great work of creation had been accomplished. And God "rested on the seventh day from all His work which He had made. And God blessed the seventh day, and sanctified it: because that in it He had rested from all His work which God created and made." God looked with satisfaction upon the work of His hands.

All was perfect, worthy of its divine Author, and He rested, not as one weary, but as well pleased with the fruits of His wisdom and goodness and the manifestations of His glory.

After resting upon the seventh day, God sanctified it, or set it apart, as a day of rest for man. Following the example of the Creator, man was to rest upon this sacred day, that as he should look upon the heavens and the earth, he might reflect upon God's great work of creation; and that as he should behold the evidences of God's wisdom and goodness, his heart might be filled with love and reverence for his Maker.

In Eden, God set up the memorial of His work of creation, in placing His blessing upon the seventh day. The Sabbath was committed to Adam, the father and representative of the whole human family. Its observance was to be an act of grateful acknowledgment, on the part of all who should dwell upon the earth, that God was their Creator and their rightful Sovereign; that they were the work of His hands and the subjects of His authority. Thus the institution was wholly commemorative, and given to all mankind. There was nothing in it shadowy or of restricted application to any people.

God saw that a Sabbath was essential for man, even in Paradise. He needed to lay aside his own interests and pursuits for one day of the seven, that he might more fully contemplate the works of God and meditate upon His power and goodness. He needed a Sabbath to remind him more vividly of God and to awaken gratitude because all that he enjoyed and possessed came from the beneficent hand of the Creator.[75]

Abraham Lincoln is quoted as saying, "As we keep or break the Sabbath day, we nobly save or meanly lose the last best hope by which man rises."[76]

Reformed Protestant theologian Karl Barth (1886–1968) wrote with depth and creative insight about the Sabbath. He considered the Sabbath not just a commandment but also a revelation of God. He extols the creation of the Sabbath, according to the Genesis account, as an essential reminder of the ancient nature and divine character of the day. The Sabbath is spoken of as rooted in God's example and is therefore far older than the Decalogue.

In writing about God's rest, Barth explains that God did not need to recuperate after a busy six days of creating. Rather, this rest suggested that God was so content and so satisfied with His work of creation that His work could now cease without regret. He had no need to go on creating, for everything was "very good." He did not stop being the Creator but needed to add nothing else. Moreover, His rest did not mean that He withdrew from it, nor departed from it as the deists claimed. The Sabbath is tied to the full completion of a "very good" creation[77] and underscores "a supremely positive relationship of God to the creaturely world and man as they now confronted Him."[78] And God Himself set His own limits in His creative activity. He is truly God standing over what He has made. God ended His creative activity because He had "found the object of His love."

> By establishing the Sabbath day, and resting on it, God indicated that He Himself enters time, that He enters into ongoing creation history and links Himself temporally "with the being and purpose and course of the world, with the history of man."

In this sense, man and woman are not the crown of creation after all; rather, the Sabbath is the pinnacle of the Genesis account, for it is the Sabbath that reveals the true character of the Creator, His freedom, His love, and His desire to continue to associate with what He made. The Sabbath represents the beginning of the history of humankind with God, the beginning of an everlasting covenant relationship. Instead of retiring into eternity [as the Deists argue], God gives temporal form to His freedom and love by entering into the seventh day."[79]

It is God who has worked and accomplished creation, this occasion for rest and joy. It is initiated solely because of what God has done, not for what the man and woman have done. Hereby the universe of grace is suggested. God has done what was necessary, and humans are granted this rich grace at the outset of their lives. . . . The Sabbath brings God's people into contact with the gospel. They cannot do justice to their work without first pausing, resting, rejoicing, and observing the Sabbath interruption of that work. In the Sabbath is "the true time" which gives meaning to the rest of time.[80]

According to Barth, what the Sabbath really forbids is not work, but trust in human work: "The aim of the Sabbath commandment is that man shall give and allow the omnipotent grace of God to have the first and the last word at every point." He speaks of the "radical importance, the almost monstrous range of the Sabbath commandment." "It confronts us with the Creator, with His will and word and work, and with the final goal determined by Him."[81]

In Chicago. Dwight L. Moody, the founder of the Moody Bible Institute, published his thoughts about the seventh day:

I honestly believe that this commandment [the Sabbath commandment] is just as binding today as it ever was. I have talked with men who have said that it has been abrogated [abolished], but they have never been able to point to any place in the Bible where God repealed it. When Christ was on earth, He did nothing to set it aside; He freed it from the traces under which the scribes and Pharisees had put it, and gave it its true place. "The Sabbath was made for men, not man for the Sabbath" (*Mark 2:27*). It is just as practicable and as necessary for men today as it ever was—in fact, more than ever, because we live in such an intense age. The [Seventh-day] Sabbath was binding in Eden, and it has been in force ever since. This Fourth Commandment [Exodus 20:8-11] begins with the word "remember," showing the Sabbath had already existed when God wrote the law on the tables of stone at Sinai. How can men claim that this one commandment has been done away with when they admit that the other nine are still binding? Dwight L. Moody, *Weighed and Wanting*, 1898, pp. 46-47.[82]

Also: "This Fourth is not a commandment for one place, or one time, but for all places and times.—D. L. MOODY, *at San Francisco, Jan. 1st*, 1881."[83]

In Rome. In 1998, the pope published a lengthy apostolic letter entitled "*Dies Domini: of the Holy Father John Paul II to the Bishops, Clergy and Faithful of the Catholic Church on Keeping the Lord's Day Holy.*"[84] The introduction firmly upholds Sunday sacredness, though undergirding it by the Creation record of Genesis 1, 2. The importance and meaning of Sabbath are strongly upheld, but not the seventh day.

Conclusion

Ellen White asserts that the true Sabbath was never lost:

Hallowed by the Creator's rest and blessing, the Sabbath was kept by Adam in his innocence in holy Eden; by Adam, fallen yet repentant, when he was driven from his happy estate. It was kept by all the patriarchs, from Abel to righteous Noah, to Abraham, to Jacob. When the chosen people were in bondage in Egypt, many, in the midst of prevailing idolatry, lost their knowledge of God's law; but when the Lord delivered Israel, He proclaimed His law in awful grandeur to the assembled multitude, that they might know His will and fear and obey Him forever.

From that day to the present the knowledge of God's law has been preserved in the earth, and the Sabbath of the fourth commandment has been kept. Though the "man of sin" succeeded in trampling underfoot God's holy day, yet even in the period of his supremacy there were, hidden in secret places, faithful souls who paid it honor. Since the Reformation, there have been some in every generation to maintain its observance. Though often in the midst of reproach and persecution, a constant testimony has been borne to the perpetuity of the law of God and the sacred obligation of the creation Sabbath.[85]

Throughout the history of the church, three main views have developed regarding the seventh-day Sabbath:

1. Some believe that "Sabbath" must always refer to the seventh day of the week, and the time for observing it on that day has never changed.

2. Some Christians believe that it is legitimate for Christians to transfer Sabbath sacredness to Sunday. Because the first day of the week was the day of Jesus' resurrection, it is fitting to worship and rest on that day. While agreeing with the first position that Christians must observe one day in seven as a day of rest and call it "Sabbath," they insist it doesn't need to be Saturday. Some even go so far as to suggest that each person can choose one day in seven that fits their schedule best.

3. Others believe that Sabbath sacredness cannot be transferred from Saturday to another day. They agree with the second position inasmuch as it is appropriate to worship on Sunday. However, they usually do not call Sunday the "Christian Sabbath," often preferring to call it "the Lord's Day" to make it clear that Sunday and Sabbath are not the same. They believe the New Testament

teaches that Sabbath laws were fulfilled in Christ in such a way that Christians are not commanded to keep one day out of seven though this may be done voluntarily. Jesus is said to have obeyed Torah because He understood it to be binding then. But Christians are now under the new covenant.

Seventh-day Adventists continue to advocate the true biblical Sabbath by deliberately naming ourselves *Seventh-day* Adventists! There is no way we can hide our conviction about which day is the biblical Sabbath!

We are not alone in this. The Bible Sabbath Association maintains a website that includes news and information about other Sabbath-keeping believers and congregations. Though we are not the only Christian denomination to keep the seventh-day Sabbath, our vital contribution is the connection of the Sabbath to the three angels' messages of Revelation 14. These proclamations, given with a "loud voice," place the Sabbath within the comprehensive salvation history parameters that commence in the Old Testament and continue throughout the New Testament—climaxing in the book of Revelation.

But does it really matter? So what? Isn't it more important to focus on the love of Jesus? These are crucial questions. Moreover, "keeping the Sabbath" sometimes ends up being a burden instead of a blessing. If not rightly understood, a Sabbath keeper may end up being a legalist—never discovering the heartbeat of the Creator and what He wanted the Sabbath to be. The final chapter of this book will tackle that issue—for it is at the heart of true Sabbath theology. But first, there are a few supposed "problem" texts that need to be studied. It is time to do this now that we have reviewed the extensive embeddedness of the Sabbath consistently found all through Scripture.

---

1. Philo, *On the Creation of the World* 30.89, 90, in F. H. Colson and G. H. Whitaker, trans., *Philo*, vol. 1, Loeb Classical Library (Cambridge, MA: Harvard University Press, 1981).

2. Philo, *On the Ten Festivals* ["The Second Festival," sec. 5], in C. D. Yonge, trans., *The Works of Philo Judaeus*, vol. 3 (London: Henry G. Bohn, 1855), 275, 276.

3. Philo, *On the Decalogue* 20, in C. D. Yonge, trans., *The Works of Philo Judaeus*, vol. 3 (London: Henry G. Bohn, 1855), 158, 159.

4. Philo, *On the Decalogue* 20.96–98, in F. H. Colson, trans., *Philo*, vol. 7, Loeb Classical Library (Cambridge, MA: Harvard University Press, 1998), 55, 57.

5. *On the Special Laws* 2.48.260, in Colson, *Philo*, 7:469, 471.

6. *On the Special Laws* 2.15.60–64, in Colson, *Philo*, 7:345, 347.

7. Tertullian, *Against Marcion* 4.12, in Alexander Roberts and James Donaldson, eds., *The Ante-Nicene Fathers*, vol. 3, American ed. (New York: Charles Scribner's Sons, 1918), 363.

8. Kenneth A. Strand, "Tertullian and the Sabbath," *Andrews University Seminary Studies* 9, no. 2 (1971): 136.

9. Strand, 136.

10. Strand, 137.

11. Strand, 137.

12. Origen, *Homilies on Numbers* 23.4.749, 750, in J. P. Migne, ed., *Patrologia Graeca*, vol. 12 (Paris: n.p., 1857); Frank H. Yost's translation, quoted in Don F. Neufeld and Julia Neuffer, eds., *The Seventh-day Adventist Bible Students' Source Book* (Washington, DC: Review and Herald®, 1962), 876.

13. Irenaeus, *Against Heresies* 4.16, in Alexander Roberts and James Donaldson, eds., *The Ante-Nicene Fathers*, vol. 1, American ed. (New York: Charles Scribner's Sons, 1913), 480.

14. Justin Martyr, *Dialogue With Trypho* 12, in Roberts and Donaldson, *The Ante-Nicene Fathers*, 1:200.

15. Theophilus of Antioch, *Theophilus to Autolycus*, book 2, ch. 11, in *Ante-Nicene Fathers*, ed., Alexander Roberts and James Donaldson, trans. Marcus Dods, vol. 2, American ed., 1885, online ed., 2004, 184.

16. Theophilus, *Theophilus to Autolycus*, book 2, ch. 12, 185.

17. Benjamin George Wilkinson, *Truth Triumphant: The Church in the Wilderness* (Rapidan, VA: Hartland Publications, 2004), 298.

18. Gary Hullquist, *Sabbath Diagnosis: A Diagnostic History and Physical Examination of the Biblical Day of Rest* (Brushton, NY: TEACH Services, 2004), 75.

19. Joseph Bingham, *Antiquities of the Christian Church*, vol. 2 (London: Henry G. Bohn, 1856), 1138.

20. Peter Heylyn, *The History of the Sabbath* (Albany, OR: Books for the Ages, 1997), 184.

21. Wilkerson, *Truth Triumphant*, 57.

22. Wilkerson, 75n15.

23. Charles Joseph Hefele, "*A History of the Councils of the Church*," vol. 2 (n.p.: Veritatis Splendor, 2014) , 362, 369.

24. Heylyn, *History of the Sabbath*, 187.

25. Hullquist, *Sabbath Diagnosis*, 119.

26. Werner Vyhmeister, "The Sabbath in Egypt and Ethiopia," in *The Sabbath in Scripture and History*, ed. Kenneth A. Strand (Washington, DC: Review and Herald®, 1982), 171.

27. Vyhmeister, "Sabbath in Egypt and Ethiopia," 171.

28. Ellen G. White, *Spirit of Prophecy*, vol. 4 (Oakland, CA, Pacific Press®, 1884), 392.

29. White, 392, 393.

30. Hullquist, *Sabbath Diagnosis*, 416.

31. Hullquist, 416. "The editor of the best biography of Columba says in a footnote: 'Our Saturday. The custom to call the Lord's day Sabbath did not commence until a thousand years later.' Adamnan's "Life of Columbia" (Dublin, 1857), p. 230." Hullquist, 416.

32. Hullquist, 416.

33. Hullquist, 416.

34. Alex Toukam, *The Sabbath* (Berlin, AZ: Alex Toukam Publishing, 2015), https://books.google.com/books?id=WGjsCgAAQBAJ.

35. Toukam, https://books.google.com/books?id=WGjsCgAAQBAJ.

36. Toukam, https://books.google.com/books?id=WGjsCgAAQBAJ.

37. Toukam, https://books.google.com/books?id=WGjsCgAAQBAJ.

38. Hullquist, *Sabbath Diagnosis*, 418.

39. Hullquist, 419.

40. Hullquist, 419.

41. Hullquist, 419.

42. Hullquist, 420.

43. Hullquist, 420.

44. Toukam, https://books.google.com/books?id=WGjsCgAAQBAJ.

45. David Benedict, *A General History of the Baptist Denomination in America, and Other Parts of the World*, vol. 2 (Boston: David Benedict, 1813), 413.

46. Toukam, *The Sabbath*, https://books.google.com/books?id=WGjsCgAAQBAJ.

47. Hullquist, *Sabbath Diagnosis*, 423.

48. Martin Luther, *Luther's Works*, vol. 44, *The Christian in Society 1*, ed. James Atkinson (Philadelphia: Fortress Press, 1966), 78.

49. Martin Luther, *Luther's Works*, vol. 52, *Sermons 2*, ed. Hans J. Hillerbrand (St. Louis, MO: Concordia, 1974), 246.

50. Martin Luther, *Luther's Works*, vol. 1, *Lectures on Genesis, Chapters 1–5*, ed. Jaroslav J. Pelikan (St. Louis, MO: Concordia, 1958), 79.

51. Luther, *Luther's Works*, 1:80.

52. P. Gerard Damsteegt, "The Sabbath and the Most Prominent Magisterial Reformers" (n.p.: Biblical Research Institute, 2011), 3, https://adventistbiblicalresearch.org/sites/default/files/pdf/Sabbath%20and%20Reformers.pdf.

53. J. N. Andrews and L. R Conradi, *History of the Sabbath*, 4th ed. (Washington, DC: Review and Herald®, 1912), 630. Translated from Erlanger edition of Luther's works, 92.

54. John Calvin, *Commentaries on the First Book of Moses Called Genesis*, vol. 1 (1554) in *Calvin Commentaries* (22 vols), trans. John King (Edinburgh: Calvin Translation Society, 1844056, repr. ed., Grand Rapids: Baker, 2005), 104.

55. Calvin, *Genesis*, 1:106.

56. Damsteegt, "Magisterial Reformers," 5.

Rediscovering the Glory the Sabbath

57. Walter B. Douglas, "The Sabbath in Puritanism," in *The Sabbath in Scripture and History*, ed. Kenneth A. Strand (Hagerstown, MD: Review and Herald®, 1982), 238.

58. John Owen, *Exercitations Concerning the Name, Oringal, Nature, Use, and Continuance of a Day of Sacred Rest* (1671), 399.

59. Edward Stennett, letter to "Sabbath-Keepers in Rhode Island," February 2, 1668, quoted in "The Seventh-Day Baptist Church in Newport, R. I.," Historical Department, *Seventh-day Baptist Memorial* 1, no. 1 (January 1852): 26.

60. Le Roy Edwin Froom, *The Prophetic Faith of Our Fathers*, vol. 4 (Washington, DC: Review and Herald®, 1954), 915.

61. Winton Solberg, *Redeem the Time: The Puritan Sabbath in Early America* (Cambridge, MA: Harvard Univ. Press, 1977), 311.

62. Hullquist, *Sabbath Diagnosis*, 428.

63. Hullquist, 428.

64. Hullquist, 428.

65. Hullquist, 428.

66. Hullquist, 430.

67. Hullquist, 430.

68. Hullquist, 430.

69. Hullquist, 429.

70. Hullquist, 429.

71. Hullquist, 430.

72. Hullquist, 430, 431.

73. Hullquist, 73.

74. *Evangelisten* (Evangelist), May 30, 1863, 169, quoted in Christian Edwardson, *Facts of Faith*, rev. ed. (Nashville, TN: Southern Pub. Assn., 1943), 175.

75. Ellen G. White, *Patriarchs and Prophets* (Mountain View, CA, Pacific Press®, 1958), 47, 48.

76. Matthew Sleeth, *24/6: A Prescription for a Healthier, Happier Life* (n.p.: Tyndale, 2012), 3.

77. Karl Barth, *Church Dogmatics*, vol. 3, pt. 1 (Edinburgh: T&T Clark, 2007), 213–228; Karl Barth, *Church Dogmatics*, vol. 3, pt. 4 (New York: T&T Clark, 2004), 47–72.

78. Barth, *Church Dogmatics*, vol. 3 part 1, 223.

79. Barth, 216, 217.

80. Barth, vol. 3, part 4, 45–51.

81. Barth, 57.

82. John Buckley, *Prophecy Unveiled: Exploring the Incredible Truths That Lie Hidden in the BIble* (n.p.: Xulon, 2007), 118, 119.

83. Wibur F. Crafts, *The Sabbath for Man: A Study of the Origin, Obligtion, History, Advantages and Present State of Sabbath Observance With Special Reference to the Rights of Workingmen* [. . .] (New York: Funk and Wagnalls, 1885), [8].

84. The document in its entirety can be found online.

85. Ellen G. White, *The Great Controversy* (Mountain View, CA, Pacific Press®, 1950), 453.

Chapter Six

What's the Problem?

We have taken time to survey how evidence for the biblical Sabbath is widely embedded in both testaments, commencing with Creation week in the divine designation and blessing of the seventh day. God used the same verbs when He repeated the account of this event in the fourth commandment of the Decalogue. The example of Jesus and the apostles in the New Testament corresponded with Old Testament teaching. The seventh-day Sabbath is consistently upheld in both testaments. These overarching parameters must be allowed to inform any texts that might not seem so clear. Yet, a few biblical texts are sometimes suggested as supporting a shift of the seventh-day Sabbath to Sunday in the New Testament. We need to look at these "problem texts."

First of all, it must be remembered that though the Bible is not a formal volume of systematic theology, it is a "system of truth." This is a crucial point. If one takes the claims of the biblical writers seriously, divine claims of Scripture must be acknowledged. God engaged various different writers over many centuries to receive and then record the revelation He gave them. The Old Testament is the oldest collection of divinely inspired "books." Jesus and the apostles fully accepted, endorsed, and taught the full authority of this "collection."*

Second, no one biblical writer, no one verse, no one chapter, no one biblical book contains or presents exhaustive truth—all that can be known or apprehended. Nor does any biblical writer contradict himself or any other biblical writer in either the Old or New Testament. One must take the entire collection of sixty-six books in its entirety as an all-inclusive unit—comparing all sixty-six books to one another when seeking to understand what Scripture is teaching. I like to think of each biblical writer and/or book contributing to a beautiful mosaic: looking closely, one sees the many distinct parts. But all have been designed to contribute to a larger, comprehensive picture.

The comprehensive picture formed by the biblical writers is the "system of truth" that God the Author created. Recognizing this is crucial for "rightly dividing the word of truth" (2 Timothy 2:15)—as Paul admonished the young pastor Timothy. It is the fundamental principle that must be acknowledged to understand what the Bible is teaching about any doctrine.

Jesus alluded to this foundational standard twice on Resurrection Sunday. The first time was on the road to Emmaus as He walked with two disciples who were distraught over His crucifixion. "Then He said to them, 'O foolish ones, and slow of heart to believe in all that the prophets have spoken! Ought not the Christ to have suffered these things and to enter into His glory?' And beginning at Moses and all the Prophets, He expounded to them in all the Scriptures the things concerning Himself" (Luke 24:25–27).

Back in Jerusalem with the main group of disciples, He referred the second time to this crucial interpretive principle: "Then He

---

* The New Testament writers often referred to different parts of the Old Testament and apparently taught believers to do the same. The testimony concerning the Berean believers suggests this: "These were more fairminded than those in Thessalonica, in that they received the word with all readiness, and *searched the Scriptures daily to find out whether these things were so*" (Acts 17:11; emphasis added).

said to them, 'These are the words which I spoke to you while I was still with you, that all things must be fulfilled which were written in the Law of Moses and the Prophets and the Psalms concerning Me.' And *He opened their understanding, that they might comprehend the Scriptures*" (Luke 24:44, 45; emphasis added).

Jesus' emphasis on this principle of interpreting the Written Word is notable. In this last case, He cited all the major Old Testament sections—Moses, the Prophets, and the Psalms—to inform His teaching about Himself and His salvific mission.

With that evidence in mind, and having spent several chapters reviewing the pervasiveness of the biblical Sabbath in both the Old and New Testaments, let's look at a few texts that are sometimes used to suggest that the biblical teaching of the seventh-day Sabbath would eventually support Sunday sacredness.

Matthew 24:20

"And pray that your flight may not be in winter or on the Sabbath."

In Matthew 24, Jesus was discussing the future with His disciples. They had asked, "What will be the sign of Your coming, and of the end of the age?" (verse 3). When Jesus responded, He did not suggest that the Sabbath wouldn't last. Pointing to the future destruction of Jerusalem—which would happen decades later—He actually taught that the biblical Sabbath would still be in place. Jesus was not announcing any change in the seventh-day Sabbath. Rather, He underscored that in the future, the seventh day would remain unchanged.

Jesus couldn't be talking about the "Jewish" Sabbath because the Sabbath was given before there were any Jews. And, as we have seen, the book of Acts records both the apostles and the Gentiles still keeping the Sabbath long after Christ's ascension. Jesus had

185

several post-Resurrection appearances on Sunday, but neither then nor at any other time during His public ministry did He suggest a possible change of the Sabbath. Nor was the Sabbath nullified by His death. The law did not cease because of the Cross. Jesus died because the law could not be changed.

2 Timothy 2:8

> Remember that Jesus Christ, of the seed of David, was raised from the dead according to my gospel, for which I suffer trouble as an evildoer, even to the point of chains; but the word of God is not chained.

If the entire chapter is read, it is very clear Paul is not urging a change of the Sabbath to Sunday. He is talking about the Jewish leaders' rejection of Jesus as the Messiah—an issue that he wasn't afraid to address. This aroused the same antagonism against him that Jesus had received—causing extreme suffering for both.

The book of Acts tells us Paul was viciously attacked for not insisting that Gentile converts be circumcised, but he was never even accused of breaking the Sabbath—which, as we have seen, would have been a high crime.*

Paul's Sabbath keeping was not a strange doctrine to first-century Gentiles. As we saw, the book of Acts describes both Jew and new Gentile believers keeping the biblical Sabbath together. Two first-century Jewish writers, Josephus and Philo, also wrote about the seventh-day Sabbath:

---

*Although circumcision was a command of God and part of the Mosaic system, Paul contrasted circumcision to the Decalogue, and in doing so separated it from the eternal law. "But as God has distributed to each one, as the Lord has called each one, so let him walk. And so I ordain in all the churches. Was anyone called while circumcised? Let him not become uncircumcised. Was anyone called while uncircumcised? Let him not be circumcised. Circumcision is nothing and uncircumcision is nothing, but keeping the commandments of God is what matters" (1 Corinthians 7:17–19).

What's the Problem?

- Josephus: "There is not one city, Greek or barbarian, nor a single nation, to which our custom of abstaining from work on the seventh day has not spread "[1]
- Philo: The Sabbath is "the festival not of a single city or country but of the universe."[2]

Romans 14:1–9

Receive one who is weak in the faith, but not to disputes over doubtful things. For one believes he may eat all things, but he who is weak eats only vegetables. Let not him who eats despise him who does not eat, and let not him who does not eat judge him who eats; for God has received him. *Who are you to judge* another's servant? To his own master he stands or falls. Indeed, he will be made to stand, for God is able to make him stand.

One person esteems one day above another; another esteems every day alike. Let each be fully convinced in his own mind. He who observes the day, observes it to the Lord; and he who does not observe the day, to the Lord he does not observe it. He who eats, eats to the Lord, for he gives God thanks; and he who does not eat, to the Lord he does not eat, and gives God thanks. *For none of us lives to himself, and no one dies to himself. For if we live, we live to the Lord; and if we die, we die to the Lord. Therefore, whether we live or die, we are the Lord's. For to this end Christ died and rose and lived again, that He might be Lord of both the dead and the living* (emphasis added).

In this Pauline passage, esteeming days is linked to issues of "eating," "not eating," and fasting. This letter is also the only time (verse 2) that Paul uses the word *laxana* (vegetables).

Apparently, this was a situation involving Roman believers, for Paul discussed this issue only with them. The passage does not

187

specify anything about the seventh-day Sabbath, though some try to make the connection. For one thing, Jews never fast on the Sabbath. Furthermore, Paul never taught anywhere that the Decalogue was no longer mandatory for Christians. He strongly upholds it, mentioning the law in his different letters to churches in different cities, but never hints that it is no longer valid. For example,

> Is the law then against the promises of God? Certainly not! For if there had been a law given which could have given life, truly righteousness would have been by the law. But the Scripture has confined all under sin, that the promise by faith in Jesus Christ might be given to those who believe. But before faith came, we were kept under guard by the law, kept for the faith which would afterward be revealed. Therefore the law was our tutor to bring us to Christ, that we might be justified by faith. But after faith has come, we are no longer under a tutor (Galatians 3:21–25).

> For when we were in the flesh, the sinful passions which were aroused by the law were at work in our members to bear fruit to death. But now we have been delivered from the law, having died to what we were held by, so that we should serve in the newness of the Spirit and not in the oldness of the letter (Romans 7:5–12).

> For by grace you have been saved through faith, and that not of yourselves; it is the gift of God, not of works, lest anyone should boast. For we are His workmanship, created in Christ Jesus for good works, which God prepared beforehand that we should walk in them (Ephesians 2:8–10).

In some of his letters, Paul even quotes from the Decalogue.

What's the Problem?

Note what he writes to the Romans: "What shall we say then? Is the law sin? Certainly not! On the contrary, I would not have known sin except through the law. For I would not have known covetousness unless the law had said, 'You shall not covet' " (Romans 7:7; see also Romans 13:8–10; 1 Corinthians 5:1–13; Ephesians 5:1–13).

He does insist, however, that legalistic obedience to the "letter of the law," a kind of "works righteousness," can never guarantee salvation. In fact, Paul brags that he had been flawless in his external conformity to the law. But when he accepted Jesus as his Savior, he realized that only grace could save him. The function of the law is to convict us of our critical need for salvation and bring us to Christ so that He can restore and save us. The Decalogue presents the standard of righteousness the Creator wants to restore in us, now being re-created in His image.

A basic theme found throughout the lengthy letter to the Romans is the universal sinfulness of humankind and the universal grace of God—and that justification comes only by faith. The sixteen-chapter epistle is divided into two sections: the theological discussion (chapters 1–11) and the ethical counsel (chapters 12–16). The first eleven chapters cannot be fully understood without the ethical applications of chapters 12–15. It is not possible to correctly interpret the epistle of Romans without the foundational principles found in the first eleven chapters. This is a good time to be reminded that whenever someone seeks to understand what Paul is teaching, the entire letter (or book) must be read. Otherwise, a misinterpretation of what Paul is saying can occur.

Paul doesn't elaborate on who "the weak in faith" are. However, he does speak of dealing kindly with them as they grow in faith—but without dismissing biblical teaching. In other letters, Paul was dealing with the Judaizers, but that doesn't seem to be the case here. Moreover, Paul can never be said to contradict himself though giving different counsels to different churches. In fact, he is sometimes referred to as a "contextual theologian" because he furnishes counsel to different churches (or pastors), addressing different Christian congregations he had established. It is inspired counsel, but Paul wasn't writing systematic theological discourses for the Christian church at large. He was dealing with various issues as they arose in churches he had established. Paul didn't specifically argue for the seventh-day Sabbath. However, that isn't surprising because it wasn't an issue that he needed to correct! Apparently, he taught the new Gentile believers about the Sabbath so thoroughly that he never had to defend it again to them later. The witness of his own Sabbath keeping we saw in the book of Acts must also be allowed to inform this issue.

1 Corinthians 16:1–3

Now concerning the collection for the saints, as I have given orders to the churches of Galatia, so you must do also: On the first day of the week let each one of you lay something aside, storing up as he may prosper, that there be no collections when I come. And when I come, whomever you approve by your letters I will send to bear your gift to Jerusalem.

This instruction mentions nothing about weekly Sabbath worship or taking up an offering on Sabbath. It is practical counsel about methodically setting aside money to help other Christians who were struggling financially. Curiously, today Orthodox Jews do not take up offerings on the Sabbath.

Colossians 2:11–17

In Him you were also circumcised with the circumcision made without hands, by putting off the body of the sins of the flesh, by the circumcision of Christ, buried with Him in baptism, in which you also were raised with Him through faith in the working of God, who raised Him from the dead. And you, being dead in your trespasses and the uncircumcision of your flesh, He has made alive together with Him, having forgiven you all trespasses, having wiped out the handwriting of requirements that was against us, which was contrary to us. And He has taken it out of the way, having nailed it to the cross. Having disarmed principalities and powers, He made a public spectacle of them, triumphing over them in it.

So let no one judge you in food or in drink, or regarding a festival or a new moon or sabbaths, which are a shadow of things to come, but the substance is of Christ.

When studied in context, this passage is not doing away with the Decalogue Sabbath. It warns against human legislation of "a festival or a new moon or sabbaths." Certain Jewish festive days were also known as sabbaths (see Leviticus 23:11, 32). The "festival or a new moon or sabbaths" mentioned in the text are possibly referring to the yearly, monthly, and weekly sequence. In this case, Paul is arguing about a perversion of festival days, not their "fulfillment."

The word *day* is not in the text, as some translations add. Neither is there a grammatical article before any of the three terms. Notably, the definite article ("the") is not found before the word "sabbaths." In this case, "sabbaths" in the passage are the ceremonial festival sabbaths. Either way, Paul can't be dismissing the Decalogue Sabbath, for, in the very next chapter, he cites the Decalogue, mentioning several of the commandments!

If then you were raised with Christ, seek those things which are above, where Christ is, sitting at the right hand of God. Set your mind on things above, not on things on the earth. For you died, and your life is hidden with Christ in God.

When Christ who is our life appears, then you also will appear with Him in glory.

Therefore put to death your members which are on the earth: fornication, uncleanness, passion, evil desire, and *covetousness*, which is *idolatry*. Because of these things the wrath of God is coming upon the sons of disobedience, in which you yourselves once walked when you lived in them.

But now you yourselves are to put off all these: anger, wrath, malice, *blasphemy*, *filthy language* out of your mouth. *Do not lie* to one another, since you have put off the old man with his deeds, and have put on the new man who is renewed in knowledge according to the image of Him who created him (Colossians 3:1–10; emphasis added).

Some try to argue that the seventh-day Sabbath is one of the ceremonial sabbaths. However, it is crucial at this point to again recall that the first Creation Sabbath was a divinely set weekly time given before sin. Thus, it bears repeating that even if Adam and Eve had never sinned, we would still have the blessing of the Sabbath! By contrast, the ceremonial sabbaths were given much later and connected with the yearly feasts. They are not weekly celebrations. All the yearly ceremonial sabbaths were divinely prescribed after sin and were yearly reminders of the "calendar" of salvation history.

Furthermore, early ancient documents have been found that speak of a "handwriting of requirements," which was a certificate of debt or promissory note that listed an owed debt. Paul used that ancient practice as an analogy of the debt of sin we owed that Jesus paid with His death on the cross.

Revelation 1:9, 10

I, John, both your brother and companion in the tribulation

and kingdom and patience of Jesus Christ, was on the island that is called Patmos for the word of God and for the testimony of Jesus Christ. I was in the Spirit on the Lord's Day, and I heard behind me a loud voice, as of a trumpet.

John describes being "in the spirit on the Lord's day." In the early second century, some of the church fathers began to talk of Sunday as the "Day of the Lord," connecting it to this verse. However, the *sola Scriptura* principle is violated when a person says that a text means what the church fathers say instead of "comparing scripture with scripture." It is not good exegetical practice to derive a meaning for a biblical text from a later time. Neither John nor Paul innovated Sunday sacredness for Gentile Christians, as we have seen. Moreover, Paul instructed that Christ's resurrection is celebrated by baptism (see Romans 6:1–14).

In the Old Testament, we are instructed that the Lord has a day! He also twice engraved in stone what He had declared about the Sabbath from Sinai (Exodus 20:8–11). The prophet Isaiah quoted the Lord calling the Sabbath "My holy day" (Isaiah 58:13). In the New Testament, Jesus calls Himself "Lord of the Sabbath" (Matthew 12:8), claiming this day as His own.

John was in the spirit on the "Lord's day" when he received his overwhelming vision of Jesus, "And *when I saw Him, I fell at His feet as dead. But He laid His right hand on me, saying to me, 'Do not be afraid;* I am the First and the Last. I am He who lives, and was dead, and behold, I am alive forevermore. Amen. And I have the keys of Hades and of Death'" (Revelation 1:17, 18; emphasis added). The rest of Scripture interprets "the Lord's day" as the biblical Sabbath.

Other objections to the seventh day being the true Sabbath for Christians in our time

1. Why can't a person keep every day, or pick the most convenient day in the week to keep Sabbath?

Response: Different Protestant traditions have suggested different ideas. Some of the Reformers determined there were no more certain holy times because there were no more holy places. The Puritans, not satisfied with this teaching about the Sabbath, chose Sunday.

Various Protestant traditions have chosen to keep Sunday sacred (1) to avoid confusion with Jewish tradition—because it was the Jews who crucified Jesus* or (2) to honor Jesus' resurrection because Jesus rose from the dead on a Sunday.

Honoring Jesus is a wonderful motivation, but Jesus clearly designated which day He made holy. Moreover, if we actually learn to "delight" in the Sabbath, we are promised that we will "delight in the Lord"!

> "If you turn away your foot from the Sabbath,
> From doing your pleasure on My holy day,
> And *call the Sabbath a delight,*
> The holy day of the LORD honorable,
> And shall honor Him, not doing your own ways,
> Nor finding your own pleasure,
> Nor speaking your own words,
> *Then you shall delight yourself in the LORD*;
> And I will cause you to ride on the high hills of the earth,
> And feed you with *the heritage of Jacob your father.*
> *The mouth of the LORD has spoken*" (Isaiah 58:13, 14;
>   emphasis added).

And the same prophet instructs us that the Sabbath will be celebrated in the future "new heaven and new earth."

> "For as the new heavens and the new earth
> Which I will make shall remain before Me," says the LORD,
> "So shall your descendants and your name remain.

---

* It is crucial to read the Gospel accounts carefully on this point: it was the religious leaders who condemned Jesus, for the people "heard Him gladly" (Mark 12:37).

What's the Problem?

And it shall come to pass
That from one New Moon to another,
And from one Sabbath to another,
All flesh shall come to worship before Me," says the Lord
    (Isaiah 66:22, 23).

2. Some argue for "pan-Sabbatism"—meaning every day is holy. They suggest, Didn't God bless all days?

Response: John Calvin, when commenting on Genesis 2, declared that the "rest" of God is available every day—God's grace is always there. However, if everything is holy (meaning set apart), then nothing is holy, or set apart. If we truly want to be with God, we will want to abide by His specifics. During Creation week and in the Ten Commandments, the seventh day is set apart as holy, not the whole week or time in general.

3. It is argued that in Genesis 2:1–3, which outlines the creation of the Sabbath day, that the verses do not include the "evening and morning" clause that is found with the other six days of Creation week. Some traditions (such as the Jehovah's Witnesses) argue that because of this, the seventh day must be symbolic time equaling seven thousand years.

Response: It must be repeated that Genesis 2:2, 3, describing the creation of the Sabbath, *does* include the second of two "numbering formulas" attached to the other six days. It includes the clause with a definite article: "And on *the seventh day* God ended His work which He had done, and He rested on *the seventh day* from all His work which He had done. Then God blessed *the seventh day* and sanctified it, because in it He rested from all His work which God had created and made" (emphasis added).

    Furthermore, the second "numbering formula" ("the seventh

day") clause is repeated three times—whereas, on the other six days, the second "numbering formula" is given only once!

4. How can we be sure that the present seventh day of the week is the same seventh day of Creation week?

Response: In fact, if it is impossible to know for sure if the present seventh day is the same as the original, it would be impossible to know for sure that Resurrection Sunday is the same Sunday of the New Testament!

The Gospel of Luke records the precise timing for Jesus' crucifixion and resurrection within a sequence of verses:

> Now behold, there was a man named Joseph, a council member, a good and just man. He had not consented to their decision and deed. He was from Arimathea, a city of the Jews, who himself was also waiting for the kingdom of God. This man went to Pilate and asked for the body of Jesus. Then he took it down, wrapped it in linen, and laid it in a tomb that was hewn out of the rock, where no one had ever lain before. *That day was the Preparation, and the Sabbath drew near.*
>
> And the women who had come with Him from Galilee followed after, and they observed the tomb and how His body was laid. Then they returned and prepared spices and fragrant oils. And *they rested on the Sabbath according to the commandment.*
>
> Now *on the first day of the week*, very early in the morning, they, and certain other women with them, came to the tomb bringing the spices which they had prepared (Luke 23:50–24:1; emphasis added).*

The "first day" *follows* the Sabbath—it is *not* the Sabbath. As we reviewed earlier, after creating the first six days, the Creator rested, blessed, and made holy the first seventh day, when His creation

---

* Chapter divisions are a late addition to the biblical texts.

What's the Problem?

"work" was completed. When He came back to this earth as Savior, He announced His public mission on a Sabbath morning. And then, after completing His work of salvation, He again rested on the Sabbath.

Biblical teaching about the Sabbath is consistent, clear, and comprehensive. All Bible writers and biblical books complement each other. But believing all this still doesn't get at the heart of what the Sabbath is about. Remember that through Isaiah, God calls us to "delight" in the Sabbath—and this will cause us to "delight in the Lord." Why doesn't just knowing the right day always lead to "delight"? Let's get to the heart of the matter in the final chapter.

---

1. Flavius Josephus, *Against Apion* 2.39, in H. St. J. Thackeray, trans., *Josephus*, vol. 1, Loeb Classical Library (New York: G. P. Putnam's Sons, 1926), 405, 407.

2. Philo, *De Opificio Mundi*, 89.

Chapter Seven

The Heart of the Matter

OK. So a person can study all the biblical texts, be fully persuaded that the seventh day is the Sabbath, and faithfully set apart the day by not working and even going to church regularly—all this and still not be "keeping the Sabbath." Really? How could this be?

On the other hand, some have decided that one must keep the Sabbath to be saved. This leads to further questions: What is the relationship between the Sabbath and salvation? Is the Sabbath something that must be done to be saved? Is keeping the Sabbath merely a matter of which day? Does delighting in the Sabbath (Isaiah 58:13, 14) come in anywhere? Is "delighting" even necessary?

At this point, it is important to recall once again that Adam and Eve were given the Sabbath before they sinned—before they had even worked. So they couldn't have been trying to keep the Sabbath to be saved or feel they earned it because of their hard work. Their very first full day was the Sabbath, where they had face-to-face fellowship with their Creator before they worked at anything!

The Sabbath still offers this same set-apart time for fellowship with the Creator—who is also our needed Redeemer. Each Sabbath grants a "breather" from a busy week to reestablish harmony with God. He could have indicated that not lying, not stealing, or not committing adultery is the most important sign of being with Him. But He chose a day. And later, with His Sabbath miracles, Jesus taught the same thing, seeking to remove the human-devised restrictions that precluded full fellowship with Him. The gift of the Sabbath is so freeing, so radical, that no human being or church committee could have thought it up. The Sabbath comes each week as consecrated proof that the Creator is loving! Just as He created us to live, breathe, eat, and work, we were created to be with Him on His Sabbath.

The Sabbath is an amazing gift. No other ancient religion had gods that gave a gift of time. But do we truly understand that *it is a gift*? Have you ever given a gift to someone and then sensed that they didn't really appreciate it? God gave His human family the unimaginable gift of Sabbath time, yet we don't always gratefully receive it. Instead, we get diverted into Sabbath rules and doctrinal rationales, making it another yoke of works. Many have never learned how to accept and celebrate this extraordinary gift of the Sabbath. Doctrinal issues are absolutely vital, but presently, rather than motivating joy and praise, the Sabbath doctrine has become stifling, rarely revealing the heart of Jesus.

Often it has been taught as something necessary for salvation instead of being a divine gift like salvation. The blessed seventh day was not created by humans, nor does it need to be earned by human effort or achievement. Nor is it a reward. It is an extraordinary gift from the Creator, who thereby demonstrated that He is sovereign even over time!

Instead of enabling us to win merit with God, the Sabbath is the bond, or seal, to keep us close to Him and a day to celebrate redemption already received. Obedience to the fourth commandment of the Decalogue should flow from the joy of being redeemed! The sequence in the narrative of Exodus makes this clear.

The Old Testament ritual calendar began with Passover. The Lord explained to Moses and Aaron: "This month shall be your beginning of months; it shall be the first month of the year to you" (Exodus 12:1, 2). He then provided instructions for celebrating Passover: that anyone who came "under the blood" could be saved. In the New Testament, Jesus is identified as "the Lamb of God" under whose shed blood we can be saved (cf. John 1:29; 1 Corinthians 5:7; Revelation 1:5; 5).

Fifty days later, the children of Israel were at Mount Sinai, where God spoke the law to them. This was the first Pentecost, coming fifty days after Passover. Note the sequence: first grace/salvation and then the giving of the law!

We could learn from the tradition of our Jewish brothers and sisters—how they *celebrate* the giving of the law each Pentecost! Rather than thinking of God's law as a burden, a "straitjacket," the Jewish tradition revels in the gift of the law every year!

Pentecost in the New Testament

The Christian understanding of "Pentecost" is usually restricted to the gift of the Holy Spirit recorded in Acts 2: "When *the Day of Pentecost had fully come*, they were all with one accord in one place. And suddenly there came a sound from heaven, as of a rushing mighty wind, and it filled the whole house where they were sitting. Then there appeared to them divided tongues, as of fire, and one sat upon each of them. And they were all filled with the Holy Spirit and began to speak with other tongues, as the Spirit gave them utterance" (Acts 2:1–4).

What happened in Acts 2 was an Old Testament type meeting its fulfillment. Paul taught the Corinthians concerning the Holy Spirit writing the Torah on the human heart: "You are our epistle written in our hearts, known and read by all men; clearly you are an epistle of Christ, ministered by us, written not with ink but by the Spirit of the living God, not on tablets of stone but on tablets of flesh, that is, of the heart" (2 Corinthians 3:2, 3).

The book of Revelation (chapter 14) presents another fulfillment of Exodus typology, which we will review later. This time, restoring the Sabbath encompasses the whole world.

Sabbath patterns

Scriptural patterns involving the Sabbath must now be noted. When apostasy emerged in God's people, the Sabbath is often involved. And when divine redemption (a type of re-creation!) was experienced, look for Sabbath restoration. For example, when freed from their deserved captivity in Babylon, Nehemiah and Ezra specifically urged not to break the Sabbath—and reminded the people that their Sabbath profanation was behind their punishing judgment (see Nehemiah 13:15–22).

As reviewed in an earlier chapter, any doctrinal study must work within the Bible's "system of truth." As this is done, it will draw attention to the fact that the various biblical teachings, or doctrines, are linked together, informing and illuminating each other. For example, note how the doctrine of the divine creation of space and time connects with other biblical doctrines:

- When the Creator set in place the weekly cycle climaxing with the Sabbath day, He established a weekly memorial of His creating this blessed world.
- When we tithe, we return to God a small portion of what He created.
- When Jesus was born, He assumed the human flesh He created.
- When He died on the cross, He died to save the lives He created.
- When He comes again, He will return to reclaim what He created.
- When we mess up and sin for six days, each Sabbath we are invited by our Creator to come to Him for healing, renewal, and forgiveness—each week, we experience a kind

of miniature eschatology—a small-scale representation of salvation history.

When these interconnections are comprehended, the Sabbath will help open our minds and hearts to the love of the Creator Jesus.

More than merely the right day
The 28 fundamental beliefs of the Seventh-day Adventist Church are more than just a set of doctrines, something like a "grocery list"—each item with a few texts supporting it. As foundational as they are in expressing what the Bible teaches, it is even more important to recognize how these biblical doctrines all work together.

For example, we are right to call attention to the importance of the seventh-day Sabbath. But the Sabbath is a lot more than not Sunday. The belief does not just present a list of texts about the Sabbath. It teaches about Jesus! Our goal is not just to convince others to keep the biblical Sabbath and join our church. Rather, our goal should be to invite others to share in our relationship with Jesus, with the Sabbath being a paramount way He provides to deepen our fellowship with Him for a whole day each week!

The Jewish leaders in Jesus' day were adamant about the seventh-day Sabbath—and they were right about which day it was and its importance. But they rejected Jesus. They did this even though Old Testament prophets had often railed against externally exemplary worship that didn't issue from a heart linked with Yahweh. Hosea tells us God rejected their Sabbath keeping even though they were worshiping on the right day:

"Therefore I will return and take away
My grain in its time
And My new wine in its season,
And will take back My wool and My linen,

Given to cover her nakedness. . . .
I will also cause all her mirth to cease,
Her feast days,
Her New Moons,
Her Sabbaths—
All her appointed feasts" (Hosea 2:9–11; emphasis added).

God's desire for fellowship with us

God did not leave behind any manuscripts that He penned. But twice, He wrote in stone with His finger the words of Decalogue. Moses records the first time God did this:

> " 'And remember that you were a slave in the land of Egypt, and the Lord your God brought you out from there by a mighty hand and by an outstretched arm; therefore the Lord your God commanded you to keep the Sabbath day.
> 'Honor your father and your mother, as the Lord your God has commanded you, that your days may be long, and that it may be well with you in the land which the Lord your God is giving you.
> 'You shall not murder.
> 'You shall not commit adultery.
> 'You shall not steal.
> 'You shall not bear false witness against your neighbor.
> 'You shall not covet your neighbor's wife; and you shall not desire your neighbor's house, his field, his male servant, his female servant, his ox, his donkey, or anything that is your neighbor's.'
> *"These words the Lord spoke to all your assembly, in the mountain from the midst of the fire, the cloud, and the thick darkness, with a loud voice; and He added no more. And He wrote them on two tablets of stone and gave them to me"* (Deuteronomy 5:15–22; emphasis added).

The second time God wrote with His own hand, He replaced the first engraved tablets that Moses broke in distress because of Israel's grave golden-calf apostasy. "And the LORD said to Moses, 'Cut two tablets of stone like the first ones, and *I will write on these tablets the words that were on the first tablets* which you broke' " (Exodus 34:1; emphasis added).

Deity never entrusted any human to write down the Decalogue. He alone inscribed the words. This underscores the sacred and eternal nature of them. Add to this, at Yahweh's instruction, only the divinely engraved tablets were placed *inside* the ark of the covenant, under the mercy seat. God instructed Moses to write down all the other laws given to Israel and then store them *outside* the ark. "So it was, when Moses had completed writing the words of this law in a book, when they were finished, that Moses commanded the Levites, who bore the ark of the covenant of the LORD, saying: '*Take this Book of the Law, and put it beside the ark of the covenant of the LORD your God*, that it may be there as a witness against you; for I know your rebellion and your stiff neck. If today, while I am yet alive with you, you have been rebellious against the LORD, then how much more after my death?' " (Deuteronomy 31:24–27, emphasis added). What more could God do to make clear the eternal importance and grandness of His law?

The joy and blessing of Sabbath

The subject of the blessing and joy of the biblical Sabbath is in the air these days in various articles and books by Christians:

- *Living the Sabbath: Discovering the Rhythms of Rest and Delight*, by Wendell Berry
- *Sabbath as Resistance: Saying No to the Culture of Now*, by Walter Brueggemann
- *Subversive Sabbath: The Surprising Power of Rest in a Nonstop World*, by A. J. Swoboda

- *Keeping the Sabbath Wholly*, by Marva Dawn
- *The Rest of God*, by Mark Buchanan
- *24/6: A Prescription for a Healthier, Happier Life*, by Matthew Sleeth and Eugene H. Peterson

Even a recent pope wrote a Sabbath document: John Paul II, *Dies Domini: On Keeping the Lord's Day Holy.**

These many writers rightly urge reconsideration of and participation in the wonderful blessing of the Sabbath. Unfortunately, they then transfer Sabbath sacredness to Sunday or suggest that a person select for their Sabbath one day in seven that best fits their personal schedule.

Curiously, Seventh-day Adventists are never asked by modern writers about our joy and delight in the Sabbath, though we have been keeping the Sabbath for more than a hundred years. No one is curious about our Sabbath joy. Could it be that though we correctly focus on the right day, many of us have never fully entered into the joy of the Sabbath? When sharing the crucial biblical teaching about which day is the Sabbath, do we stop short of describing the blessing, joy, and restoration in Jesus that God intended for the seventh day? Are we silent about the "delight" of the Sabbath because we often haven't experienced it yet ourselves?

We rightly draw attention to the Sabbath by calling our denomination *Seventh-day* Adventists. Other Christian denominations also highlight important beliefs for them in their name, such as the Baptists, who affirm that the Bible teaches "believer baptism," and the Methodists, who honor John Wesley's "method" of small group ministries to ground new converts.

In our evangelistic series, we faithfully and rightly teach the biblical Sabbath and which day of the week it is. That is crucial and must not be neglected. However, Sabbath is a lot more than

---

* This document can be found free online.

not Sunday! Nor is the fourth commandment in a sequence of ten merely a long, strong, burdensome imperative. Nor was it ever meant to be something we have to do to prove our loyalty to God. Instead, it is the divine invitation into a royal way of life! It is given to us just like salvation. In fact, it is a supreme proof that God is love—for lovers like to set special times to be together!

The biblical teaching of the Sabbath prohibits work on the seventh day, but it does not prohibit great joy on the Sabbath. Work for six days is commanded: "six days you shall labor." However, God even intended work to be one of the joys of life. Adam and Eve were given work before they sinned; thus, it wasn't part of the curse of sin—though their work would be harder. Nor is the Sabbath commandment instructing people to rest so they can work. Rather, work itself is to be a blessing—followed by the crowning blessing of the Sabbath.

The seven-day weekly cycle is the divine plan for a blessed rhythm of life. We are given an alternative to modern culture's striving for success without any breaks. In fact, one of the meanings of the word *Shabbat* is to "cease from working." The unique Sabbath day helps us break away from the "works-righteousness" compulsion of modern culture. Yet, at the same time, work is valued. Work itself is a blessing—and blest are those who find joy in their work. This can be seen in the Creator's joy: each day of the first week He crowned His work with His personal declaration of "good"—and finally "very good" on day six:

"Genesis opens with the Lord creating this wonderful nest we live in—with Him exclaiming joy over the results. Then land animals, humans, and marriage were created on the sixth day—and the Creator declared, 'Very good.' Thereupon on the seventh day, the Sabbath was created, and the Lord proclaimed, 'Holy.' "[1]

The first six days are divinely "certified" as "very good." The next day was different: God declared it "holy." The first thing God made holy in the newly created world was not a mountain, nor a tree, nor a cave, but time. This indicated His personal presence in time. Recall Moses' experience at the burning bush in the wilderness. He went to see the strangely burning bush, drawing close to examine the phenomenon:

> So he looked, and behold, the bush was burning with fire, but the bush was not consumed. Then Moses said, "I will now turn aside and see this great sight, why the bush does not burn."
>
> So when the LORD saw that he turned aside to look, God called to him from the midst of the bush and said, "Moses, Moses!"
>
> And he said, "Here I am."
>
> Then He said, "*Do not draw near this place. Take your sandals off your feet, for the place where you stand is holy ground.*" Moreover, He said, "I am the God of your father—the God of Abraham, the God of Isaac, and the God of Jacob." *And Moses hid his face*, for he was afraid to look upon God (Exodus 3:2–6; emphasis added).

Moses recognized that God's glistering presence exudes holiness—a holiness that can also be present in time.

Time and the Sabbath

Structuring of time is one of the first components of the newly created order as Genesis opens. It was put in place before any living beings, human or nonhuman. The creation of measured time is emphasized. From the outset, God proved He is sovereign over all reality, including time itself, which the Sabbath certainly certifies.

"Nobody reading the panoramic prologue of Genesis can miss the structural fact which gives the text its most obvious arrangement: the framework of the seven days."[2]

Rediscovering the Glory the Sabbath

Creation, teeming with resplendent life of all kinds, was shaped within time—the first seven-day week! God climaxed that first week with the seventh-day Sabbath because the Sabbath is a blessing that all life must have to flourish. Think of it: the Sabbath is given for us to be fully human, created in God's image! God rested on the first seventh day. We surely are not stronger or smarter than our Creator. How could we possibly think we know better? If we go against the grain of the world's seven-day week, we will get splinters.[3]

Most people take the seven-day week for granted. This is understandable because it is found around the world. But it is not astronomically based like all other measurements of time, such as the 24-hour day, the 30/31-day month, or the 365/366-day year. As Genesis opens, the seven-day week is established by the Creator despite having no connection to any celestial movements. It was one of God's original creative acts.

During that first week, the Creator established all the laws of life, such as chemistry, biology, and physics. He created the atmosphere, the soil, and seas—then filled the air, waters, and soil with life. On day six, after forming the land animals and the first humans, He described the delicious diet He had created for them to eat, and then exclaimed: "Ahhh, very good! *Tov m'od!*"

Everything had been created out of nothing. God even created the animals and humans out of the soil He had made from nothing. "And the LORD God formed man of the dust of the ground, and breathed into his nostrils the breath of life; and man became a living being" (Genesis 2:7). "Out of the ground the LORD God formed every beast of the field and every bird of the air" (verse 19). The first days steadily progressed—the narrative seeming to be building up toward something grand: "the origin, and the goal not merely of human history, but of cosmic history."[4] But at the sunset of the sixth day, God did something different. He created holy time. He rested and blessed the seventh day, setting in place a distinctive rhythm of time: first six days of work, to be followed by rest and blessing on day seven. After finishing the creation of all matter and life, God rested in joy.[5] And He extended His gift to all creation—a full day to rest and enjoy His creation with Him.

How easy it is to misunderstand this and squander such a beneficent gift by trying to earn it or earn salvation by keeping it. Protestant theologian Karl Barth provides this insightful commentary: "That God rested on the seventh day and blessed and sanctified it, is the first divine action which man is privileged to witness; and that he himself may keep the Sabbath with God, completely free from work, is the first Word spoken to him, the first obligation laid on him."[6]

The only thing Adam and Eve could celebrate on that first Sabbath was their Creator, His goodness, and the newly created world. They hadn't started working yet. It cannot be stressed too often that no one must work to earn God's favor. Rather, we, too, can rest because God is already pleased with all He has accomplished.

The Sabbath reminds us of our true dignity and source. Ceasing from our weekly work, we are reminded of our benevolent Creator. Unlike most modern culture that numbly staggers on, we, in response to the divine invitation, can put a limit on our labor so that it need not become compulsive drudgery.

God's unchangeable day of rest
The seven-day week is something that should not be tinkered with, although some have tried. In 1793, France, seeking to increase human productivity, altered its calendar—extending the seven-day week to ten days. New clocks were invented to accommodate this. However, the experiment clearly failed: people burned out, production decreased, and suicide rates soared. It was learned that humans were not made to work nine days and rest only one day in ten.

Scientists are increasingly acknowledging this. "In 1974, nearly halfway through the eighty-four-day mission aboard the Skylab space station, Colonel William Pogue requested a day of rest from mission control for his overworked and exhausted space crew: 'We have been over-scheduled. We were just hustling the whole day. The work could be tiresome and tedious, though the view is spectacular.' . . . Even a breathtaking view from space cannot relieve the human need for rest." At first, NASA refused. The crew then went on strike in space! "Disobeying orders, they took a space Sabbath. In response, ground control was forced to change their policy. To this day, NASA now schedules time for rest on all space travel."[7]

Our 24/7 world is not going to change. Life only gets more intense, providing new ways to multitask—increasing the number of tasks we can do at the same time. This situation suggests that if we choose to keep the Sabbath, it will because we have made a conscious choice to do so. Resting on the Sabbath involves accepting the day of commanded rest.

If we choose to accept authentic Sabbath rest, we will more appreciate the value of rest for everyone, including the animals and even the earth. For the Decalogue's fourth commandment includes everyone—indeed, all creation. The commandment specifically includes animals in its blessing. It can also help us loosen our grim grip on our work in our present culture that sees Sabbath less and less like a welcome gift. Every seventh day we can choose to rest in God's finished work, reminding us that we are saved by grace!

Many do not find it easy to take time off from their work. We are sometimes slow to admit that we are attempting to work out our salvation. We need to be reminded that God is the author *and* finisher of our faith (Hebrews 12:2): "On this day we are to celebrate, rejoice, and be free, to the glory of God. . . . This precedes talk of work—we must hear the Gospel before we can understand the law. . . . We can't value and do justice to work except in the light of its boundary, its solemn interruption—the true time from which alone we can have other work time."[8]

Our loving God is the giver of rest

Like an architect designing the many parts of a building that need to work together, God demonstrated His magnificent architectural skills as He structured creation. He first built the foundation of light, then separated water and air, after that brought out dry land. Next, He filled the different habitats with life, as we reviewed earlier—all needing the "life support" rhythms, such as circadian rhythms, seasonal changes, twenty-four-hour days.

The climax came in Genesis 2:1–3. It is fascinating to note that in the original language of these verses, there are three sentences of seven Hebrew words each—with the middle word of each sentence being the word for the seventh day. This remarkable literary feat doesn't show up in English. However, "the seventh day" is still highlighted by repetition: "Thus the heavens and the earth, and all the host of them, were finished. And on *the seventh day*, God ended His work which He had done, and He rested on *the seventh day* from all His work which He had done. Then God blessed *the seventh day* and sanctified it, because in it He rested from all His work which God had created and made" (Genesis 2:1–3; emphasis added).

In ancient times, modern techniques of italicizing, bolding, or underlining words were not available to highlight or emphasize an important idea, detail, or concept in written scripts. Rather, writers would repeat for emphasis. In that way, the remarkable repetition in Genesis 2:1–3 underscores that the seventh day is the goal of Creation! Some assume that the creation of human beings is the climax. However, the literary aspects of the text underscore that the Sabbath day is the climax, for it has more verbs connected with it than any of the other six days. Count them!

- finishing
- blessing

- resting
- making it holy

The Bible offers a view of God entirely unlike the gods of any other ancient religion. No other god or gods

- gave rest,
- beckoned any human to enjoy fellowship with them, or
- cared about the well-being of all creation, as did the God of Scripture.

The Jewish people were not the only religious people in the ancient world. The ancient Near-Eastern Akkadians, Egyptians, and Phoenicians also had their own origin myths that describe people being created to work to the bone in obedience to the fiats and commands of the gods. Unlike these other gods, however, Yahweh commanded humans to work, yes, but they must rest first! Imagine what an impression about the true God that would have given to the Akkadians, Egyptians, Phoenicians, and other ancient nations. This was a God who *commands rest*! The Genesis Creation narrative was a rebuttal of all the other "gods" who never permitted anything like this.

When one compares the biblical Creation story with these other origin accounts, several critical differences are obvious:

- The biblical Creation chronicle is the only one that presents matter—creation itself, human beings, animals, and everything else in it—as intrinsically good. In other creation myths, the world is essentially bad or evil.[9]
- Among all the ancient societies, no other sacred text held such a high view of women as the Hebrew Bible: "Let *them* [both Adam and Eve, not just Adam] have dominion" (Genesis 1:26). In the ancient records, males (rulers and

kings) alone bore their gods' image; however, the Genesis Creation account describes a world in which both male and female are created in God's image, and equal.[10]

- The Genesis Creation account, when compared with all other ancient worldviews and the origin texts of all other religions received and understood on their own terms, is singular. No other has its positive definition of human nature, human freedom, rest, women, verifiable history, and opposition to tyrannical rule.

Something particularly important about the character of God was revealed on that first seventh day: God stopped His work, but not because He was weary after creating for six days and needing to rest. Rather, He rested in pleasure and joy because of what He had accomplished. Adam and Eve's first impression of God would have been that He is not a tyrant. We are still reminded of that each week when we take a day to rest in God's presence. Sabbath is the divinely scheduled weekly reminder that we are deeply loved.

The Sabbath and the gospel proclaim the same thing! We don't have to work first to finally get rewarded with rest. God is not a slave driver, and we are not His slaves. We don't have to work to earn a day off. Rather, we are commanded to rest with God and enjoy with Him His gift of Sabbath.

Rest from slavery

As mentioned in an earlier chapter, Ellen White described how the Sabbath, when the Hebrews were slaves in Egypt, was almost lost because of the rigors of slavery. She then discussed how the first thing Moses did, when returning to Egypt, was to restore the Sabbath. This angered Pharaoh, for Egyptian pharaohs thought they were gods. And this pharaoh was used to forcing slaves to toil seven days a week.

But God delivered His people and brought them into the

wilderness to remind them—and the rest of the human race—about rest. What better time to do this than after four hundred years of slavery!

- What better time to relearn about the true God after living in Egypt, which had hundreds of gods!
- What better way to demonstrate that Pharaoh was under a delusion that he was an immortal god? Even after the ten plagues, each plague having discredited one of the Egyptian gods, he was bold enough to defy the true God!
- What better time to be reminded that God was like a loving parent! For the next forty years, God provided "angels' food" for them to eat:

> He had commanded the clouds above,
> And opened the doors of heaven,
> Had rained down manna on them to eat,
> And given them of the bread of heaven.
> Men ate angels' food;
> He sent them food to the full (Psalm 78:23–25).

Their miracle manna meals marked off each week with Sabbath rest!

- He cared for their comfort by shading them from the intense desert sun during the day and giving them light at night.

Then at Sinai came the dramatic presentation of the Decalogue and the setting up of corporate worship. The psalmist referred to this when describing Israel's sanctuary worship which commenced in the wilderness:

> Behold, how good and how pleasant it is

The Heart of the Matter

For brethren to dwell together in unity!

It is like the precious oil upon the head,
Running down on the beard,
The beard of Aaron,
Running down on the edge of his garments.
It is like the dew of Hermon,
Descending upon the mountains of Zion;
For there the LORD *commanded the blessing—*
Life forevermore (Psalm 133; emphasis added).

People do not often think about what their favorite commandment is because commandments are not generally viewed positively. The fourth commandment of the Decalogue commands remembering the Sabbath—but God was commanding *a blessing*, according to the psalmist! How much have we lost by not recognizing the Sabbath's exceptional blessing? Why have people viewed Sabbath as a duty, another work to please God, rather than accepted it as a divine gift?

Genesis chapter one repeatedly records God declaring the *goodness* of everything He made. This Creation goodness points to an important aspect of Sabbath time: the need to delight in and reflect on the goodness of what God made. The great Reformer Martin Luther saw this: "God writes the Gospel not in the Bible alone, but also on trees, and in the flowers and clouds and stars."[11]

Think of the most delicious fruit that you enjoy, say a tree-ripened mango, a ripe red strawberry, a crisp apple, or maybe a juicy watermelon. Something so delicious is good because the Creator is good! And His goodness is reflected in everything He made. For example, food didn't have to taste *this* good! The Creator obviously wanted us to enjoy eating, for He also designed our tongues with a collection of numerous and different taste buds so that we can fully delight in the many wonderful flavors of the all the foods that He thought up for us to eat! Most people never tire of eating. Obviously, this is what God had in mind when He created such an extensive "menu"! And these mouth-watering flavors are merely a foretaste of heaven to come. Listen to the final words of the Christian English martyr John Bradford, who cried out as he was about to be burned at the stake: "Look at Creation—look at it all! This is the world God has given to His enemies; imagine the world He will give *to His friends*."[12]

What about "delighting in the Sabbath, in the Lord?"
Isaiah 58:13 quotes God instructing us to call the Sabbath a "delight"—the word translated "delight" in the original language means a "royal delight." One Jewish writer called the Sabbath a "palace in time" because of this.[13] It's a "place" we can enter wherever we are. And having "delightful Sabbaths" is much different from accepting the Sabbath as being useful or something we "should do." It is a weekly lesson reminding us that our hearts can again be restored in God's great love. Amid all the stress and struggles of life, He commands us to take off fifty-two days a year and rest—wanting us to rest a seventh of our lives!

We will never truly enjoy the sacred day of rest as long as we think about it in the negative—such as "*you can't* work on the Sabbath." How much better to think this way: "*I don't have to* work on the Sabbath." Sabbath is often "worked at" with the attitude of doing stuff *for* God rather than *being with* God. Many have decided that working for God is what Sabbath is all about. Others worry that they are *breaking* the Sabbath, always trying to figure out what to do or not to do on the Sabbath. Perhaps we should wonder more whether we are *wasting* the Sabbath.

Because it has been easy to misunderstand what Sabbath is all about, thankfully, Jesus came and showed us. And what did He do? As we saw, the minute Jesus commenced His ministry on earth, He staked His claim on the Sabbath, declaring Himself the Lord of the Sabbath (Matthew 12:8). Then He sought to reteach the true meaning of the day (Luke 4:21). The gospels often record Jesus keeping the Sabbath. It is a major part of the record of His life. Many of Jesus' miracles and discussions took place on the Sabbath, for Sabbath is all about miracles and restoration. Watch Jesus set the tone, trying to recover its joy and beauty by removing the legalistic restrictions that had wrongly been added by the religious leaders in their misguided attempts to guard the sacredness of the Sabbath. He cast out demons (Luke 4:31–37), cured blindness (John 9), healed paralysis (Luke 6:6–11), straightened a crippled back (Luke 13:10–16), and rebuked a high fever (Luke 4:38, 39). He also discussed the issue with the Pharisees one Sabbath in a grainfield. Of course, one shouldn't go to all the hard work of harvesting grain on the Sabbath, but feeding the hungry was appropriate.

As we saw, the fourth commandment even lists animals among those being blessed by the Sabbath! Jesus, the "firstborn of every creature" (Colossians 1:15, KJV), did not cancel or neglect mercy for the animals: He spent His first nights with them, sleeping in a manger—an animal feeding trough. We sometimes overlook or are insensitive to the wider community of life we share with God's creation. Sabbath provides a weekly opportunity to appreciate the bonds we have with all life that comes from God's hands. We need to be reminded to treasure all nonhuman animals as Jesus did. He even notices when a sparrow falls. Animals are part of the "society" provided by the Creator—and we can hurt them by our actions. After all, we're all made from the same "stuff!" Ellen White puts it this way:

God gave to men the memorial of His creative power, that they might discern Him in the works of His hand. The Sabbath bids us behold in His created works the glory of the Creator. And it was because He desired us to do this that Jesus bound up His precious lessons with the beauty of natural things. On the holy rest day, above all other days, we should study the messages that God has written for us in nature. We should study the Saviour's parables where He spoke them, in the fields and groves, under the open sky, among the grass and flowers. As we come close to the heart of nature, Christ makes His presence real to us, and speaks to our hearts of His peace and love.[14]

Think of the benefits all animals and even the soil would receive if everyone kept the Sabbath. Moreover, the Lord promised He can heal our broken hearts and damaged souls—and He uses nature to do this. The healing benefits of nature are presently more and more recognized in such books as *Forest Therapy*, *The Hidden Lives of Trees*, and *Animal Matters: A Biologist Explains Why We Should Treat Animals With Compassion and Respect*.[15] Long ago, Ellen White wrote about the healing properties of forests of pine or hemlock.[16] She also spoke of the protective aspects of Sabbath and nature:

> If Adam and Eve had contemplated the works of God in creating the world, if they had considered the reason that God had in giving them the Sabbath, if they had looked upon the beautiful tokens he had given them in withholding nothing that would add to their happiness, they would have been safe, they would have adored him for his goodness and love toward them, and in place of listening to the sophistries of Satan in casting blame upon God, in ascribing to him motives of selfishness, they would have considered the works of his hands, and songs of melody and thanksgiving and praise would have burst forth from their lips in adoration of him who had bountifully supplied them with every good thing. If they had considered how he had made them the object of his

218

overflowing love, they would not have fallen; but they forgot the presence of God. They forgot that angels surrounded them to guard them from every danger, and they looked away from their great Benefactor.[17]

It's not so much that we keep the Sabbath as that the Sabbath keeps us!

When was the last time you praised God in a place where nothing made by humanity was around—when all you could see was God's creation? When time is taken to do this, its richness and blessing can open our hearts and minds, helping to ease a week of stress.

If our Sabbaths included such a blessing, it might inspire our caring for God's wondrous creation during the rest of the week: recycling, composting, turning out lights when leaving a room, choosing to eat a violence-free, plant-based diet, and making other caring choices. On each Sabbath, we could then more truly and honestly celebrate the great Creator!

Sabbath is meant to be a refuge, not a burden, not a prison. The Pharisees tried to "guard" it with many rules. And guarding the Sabbath is a good thing, but it should come from the positive motive of not wanting to miss a minute of its blessings! When all we think about are what rules need to be in place, it often counteracts or blocks God's wonderful purpose—causing us to lose track of His intent.

All our choices of what to do or what not to do should be made on the basis of seeking precious fellowship with Jesus and not letting anything interrupt that. Fellowship with Jesus is the primary antidote to cheerless rule-keeping often associated with the Sabbath. Often, it is not that we don't love Him; we just don't know how to spend time with Him anymore. We know Jesus is the Creator but fail to remember that He is Lord of the Sabbath as well. We can be busy working, even working for Him, and miss having fellowship with Him. Sabbath gives us time to hear the heartbeat of our Creator—a full day when we can set aside all our stress and truly rest in Jesus. After all, He issued the invitation to do just that: "Come unto me, all ye that labor and are heavy laden, and I will give you rest. Take my yoke upon you, and learn of me; for I am meek and lowly in heart: and ye shall find *rest unto your souls*" (Matthew 11:28, 29, KJV).

The Sabbath commandment begins with the *imperative* to "remember" so that we won't forget how good it is to rest in the Lord, to be loved by Him, able to hear His heartbeat. Maybe we need to be reminded of how easy it is to forget.

Maybe it isn't so much wrong intentions that cause the problem. Perhaps some have never learned to see the joy of Sabbath. Only when we have a need, recognize it, and acknowledge our inability to fulfill it can we begin to grasp our dependence on God and be truly thankful for His gracious gifts.

Sabbath rest is not given to remind us of our sinfulness but to remind us of how and why we were created: as living human beings made in God's image from the foundation of the world—made to rest in God on Sabbath. Sabbath rest is no sign of weakness or sin. God Himself rested, and it was not because He was weak!

Violating this blessed rest time is not like breaking the twenty-five mile per hour speed limit in a residential area or breaking the speed limit on the freeway when there is no police officer in sight. It is more like trying to violate the law of gravity. God created gravity. It is not just a law invented by some scientist. It is actually part of the reality we live in. Gravity is the law, and we need to obey it! Our belief or disbelief in the law of gravity will not change or invalidate it. Gravity will always win. Humans can voluntarily wreck their lives by disobeying the divine laws. We are free to do this, but the result will ultimately be deadly.

Just so with the Sabbath. Our need for Sabbath rest is like

gravity. It is the law! Our feelings and opinions cannot change it. Human beings need its blessing, and so do animals. Even the land needs it—as God insisted in the Old Testament, giving the soil a sabbatical every seven years. We may choose to ignore the Sabbath for a while, but, like gravity, it is dangerous to ignore reality. If we cling to our frantic workaholic schedules and do not rest, we will not be well. We might be fine for a while. But over time, our minds, hearts, bodies, and souls will pay a hefty price for not accepting the blessing. We can violate God's commands, but doing so will cause suffering and grave consequences.

When we do accept Sabbath rest, we will experience something incredible because the need for Sabbath rest is built into us. Jesus told us that He is "Lord of the Sabbath" (Matthew 12:8) and promised that His rest will restore us. And when we allow ourselves to accept that holy rest, it is like reentering Eden. Ellen White describes "the blessed days of Eden when God pronounced all things 'very good.' Then marriage and the Sabbath had their origin, twin institutions for the glory of God in the benefit of humanity. . . . That which the eternal Father Himself had pronounced good was the law of highest blessing and development for man."[18] "There were two institutions founded in Eden that were not lost in the fall,—the Sabbath and the marriage relation. These were carried by man beyond the gates of paradise."[19]

Holy time

The first thing God made holy during Creation was *holiness in time* on the seventh day. With His final creative act, God fashioned a holy day ("holiday") of rest. Adam and Eve didn't make the Sabbath holy—neither can we. Humans cannot make anything holy. The first humans were to *keep* the Sabbath holy, separate from all the other days.

After sin in Eden, drastic changes affected both men and women and even the soil. But the Sabbath was created before sin—and it never changed. Even if Adam and Eve had never sinned, we would still have the Sabbath! And after the curse of sin is removed, we are promised that Sabbath will continue!

"For as the new heavens and the new earth
Which I will make shall remain before Me," says the LORD,
"So shall your descendants and your name remain.
And it shall come to pass
That from one New Moon to another,
And from one Sabbath to another,
All flesh shall come to worship before Me," says the LORD
    (Isaiah 66:22, 23).

Just like salvation, Sabbath is a gift of divine grace. It is not produced by any human effort. It is not something we create or achieve—nor is it a reward. It doesn't come because we deserve it or earned it. It is a gracious gift to remind us who to thank and praise for life and salvation. Keeping the seventh day is more than fulfilling a commandment. It is a welcoming of rest in the Creator who is also our Savior: a rest *from* our busy world and a rest *in* the Creator's love. The Sabbath is more than not working. It is a time to be restored and healed. It structures a whole way of life. It reminds us of our dependency on God and even enables us to better care for the world. It is an intentional time to relearn the trustworthiness of God's timing and rejoice in it. It provides a priceless opportunity for corporate worship with other believers, allowing six days of drivenness and tension to peel away. How we understand, keep, or ignore the Sabbath will reflect our understanding of who the Creator is.

Keeping Sabbath is a revolutionary act: it defines the nature of work and creates a "sanctuary in time." It frees us to recognize and accept our birthright of being made in the image of God, and to refuse the temptation to concede to any lesser status.

The Heart of the Matter

I'm a fourth-generation Sabbath keeper and have felt pretty secure in my "Sabbath keeping." It wasn't until our family was living in Israel while my husband was studying Hebrew that my eyes and heart were finally opened to the blessed joy and royal nature of the day. Some Jewish friends invited us to celebrate the beginning of the Sabbath with them—and that changed everything. Their tradition included a festive meal on Friday night, mothers praying over their family with the lighting of Sabbath candles, dads blessing their children. Some even started thirty minutes early so they couldn't possibly miss a minute. And at the end of the blessed hours, they were reluctant to let the Sabbath go because life couldn't get better! This reminded me of how often I would watch the clock waiting for the Sabbath to end so I could get on with "my work," not at all reluctant to let the Sabbath end.

All this stopped me in my tracks. Oh, yes, I had been keeping the right day, the right hours, and doing my best! But finally, I realized that I was missing the delight in the day that promised a richer "delighting in the Lord." I hadn't wanted to spend the money it would cost to go to Israel as a family. But there, I finally realized I needed to learn much more about the love of the Lord of the Sabbath and the blessing of His royal day.

The ancient Jewish philosopher Philo wrote that the Sabbath was the "birthday of the world." We humans celebrate our birthdays once a year. But the Creator wanted us to receive and celebrate His blessings more often than that and set in place the weekly Sabbath! Every seven days, we should wish each other *Happy Birthday*!

---

1. See Matthew Sleeth, *24/6: A Prescription for a Healthier, Happier Life* (Carol Stream, IL: Tyndale House, 2012), xiv.

2. Henri Blocher, *In the Beginning: The Opening Chapters of Genesis*, trans. David G. Preston (Downers Grove, IL: InterVarsity, 1984), 39.

3. Adapted: "If you go against the grain of the universe, you get splinters." H. H.

Farmer, quoted in Eugene Peterson, *A Long Obedience in the Same Direction: Discipleship in an Instant Society*, 2nd ed. (Downers Grove, IL: InterVarsity, 2000), 109.

4. Lesslie Newbigin, *The Open Secret: An Introduction to the Theology of Mission* (Grand Rapids, MI: Eerdmans, 1995), 30, 31.

5. Paraphrased from Timothy Keller's sermon, "How to Change—Part III," *The Timothy Keller Sermon Archive* (NY: Redeemer Presbyterian Church, 2013).

6. Karl Barth, *Church Dogmatics*, vol. 3, part 1, ed. G. W. Bromiley and T. F. Torrance (New York: Charles Scribner's Sons, 1957), 216, 219.

7. A. J. Swoboda, *Subversive Sabbath: The Surprising Power of Rest in a Nonstop World* (Grand Rapids, MI: Brazos, 2018), https://books.google.com/books?id=NmAy-DwAAQBAJ.

8. Karl Barth, *Church Dogmatics*, vol. 3, pt. 4.

9. Thorkild Jacobsen contrasts Genesis with the Mesopotamian creation myth "Eridu Genesis," in which "things were not nearly as good to begin with as they have become since." In the Genesis Creation narrative, however, "things began as perfect from God's hand." Thorkild Jacobsen, "The Eridu Genesis," *Journal of Biblical Literature* 100, no. 4 (1981): 529.

10. James M. McKeown, *Genesis* (Grand Rapids, MI: Eerdmans, 2008), 279.

11. Mrs. Andrew Charles, "Hearth and Home," in *The Lutheran Witness*, ed. Martin J. Heinicke (St. Louis: Concordia, 1917).

12. Swoboda, *Subversive Sabbath.*

13. Abraham Joshua Heschel, *The Sabbath: Its Meaning for Modern Man*, FSG Classics (New York: Farrar, Straus and Giroux, 2005), 21.

14. Ellen G. White, *Christ's Object Lessons* (Washington, DC: Review and Herald®, 1941), 25, 26.

15. Ellen White speaks eloquently: "God gave the Sabbath as a memorial of his creative power and works. . . . He made its observance obligatory upon man, in order that he might contemplate the works of God, dwell upon his goodness, his mercy, and love, and through nature look up to nature's God. If man had always observed the Sabbath, there would never have been an unbeliever, and infidel, or an atheist in the world." Ellen G. White, "The Test of Loyalty," *Signs of the Times*, February 13, 1896.

16. Ellen G. White, *Manuscript Releases*, vol. 9 (Silver Spring, MD: Ellen G. White Estate, 1990), 283.

17. White, "The Test of Loyalty."

18. Ellen G. White, *The Adventist Home* (Nashville, TN: Southern Publishing Association, 1952), 341.

19. Ellen G. White, "The Creation Sabbath," *Signs of the Times*, February 28, 1884, 130.